Native peoples teach that the ultimate norm for morality is the impact our choices have on persons living seven generations from now. If the results appear good for them, then our choices are moral ones; if not, they are immoral.

We therefore dedicate Habits of Mind: A Developmental Series to our children, our grandchildren, and their children's children.

HABITS OF MIND: A DEVELOPMENTAL SERIES

Habits of Mind Web site: http://www.habits-of-mind.net/

Habits of Mind Student Book Lists: available at
http://www.ascd.org (search for "Habits of Mind:
A Developmental Series"; a link to the book lists
appears in the description)

ACTIVATING AND ENGAGING HABITS OF MIND

Applications of Habits of Mind in the Subject Areas

SERIES FOREWORD: THINKING ON THE ROAD OF LIFE

DAVID PERKINS

While driving into town a few years ago, I found myself behind a young man in a red convertible. Like many people, I have certain expectations about young men in red convertibles, but this young man surprised me. When we reached a railroad crossing, he was painfully careful. He slowed down as he approached the tracks. The closer he got to the tracks, the more he slowed. As his car passed over the tracks, it hardly was moving at all. At this point, with great care, the young man looked to the left, and then he looked to the right. No train was coming. Satisfied with his safety, he gunned the engine and sped off. The young man was careful—and yet he wasn't! Surely, the middle of the tracks isn't the best position from which to scan for oncoming trains!

This man's behavior provides a kind of a metaphor for the mission of the four-book series Habits of Mind: A Developmental Series. When on the road of life, we ought to be thoughtful about what we are doing. For example, we ought to manage impulsivity and strive for accuracy, two of the worthwhile habits of mind this series describes. Yet if good thinking is to help us out in life, it has to go on the road with us. The trouble is, good thinking often gets left behind altogether, or it's exercised in flawed ways that don't do the job, as this young man demonstrated.

How can we encourage ourselves and others—particularly students—to take good thinking on the road? Habits of Mind: A Developmental Series explores one answer to that challenge: the cultivation of habits of mind, or habits of thought as John Dewey (1933) called them. The idea is that we should have habits of mind such as persistence and flexible thinking, just as we have habits like brushing our teeth or putting the dog out or being kind to people. Habits are not behaviors we pick up and lay down whimsically or arbitrarily. They are behaviors we exhibit reliably on appropriate occasions, and they are smoothly triggered without painstaking attention.

The very notion of habits of mind, however, poses a conceptual puzzle. By definition, habits are routine, but good use of the mind is not. The phrase habits of mind makes for a kind of oxymoron, like "loud silence" or "safe risk." Indeed, the story of the young man in the convertible illustrates what can go wrong with cultivating habits of mind. Here you have a habit of mind (being careful) played out in a way that misses the point (the man looks for the train from the middle of the tracks!). The very automaticity of a habit can undermine its function. Habits like that don't serve us well on a literal highway—or on the metaphorical road of life, either.

Can one have a habit of mind that truly does its work? The resolution to this puzzle is not very difficult. There's a difference between the thinking required to manage a mental process and the thinking done by the process. A habitual mental process does not require a lot of management to launch and sustain it, but that process itself may conduct mindful thinking. It may involve careful examination of alternatives, assessment of risks and consequences, alertness to error, and so on. For example, I have a simple, well-entrenched habit for the road of life: looking carefully when I depart a setting to be sure that I'm not leaving anything behind. This habit triggers and runs off reliably, with very little need for mindful management. But the behaviors deployed by the habit are highly mindful: scrutinizing the setting, glancing under chairs for concealed objects, and peering into drawers and closets for overlooked items.

In all fairness, the man in the convertible displayed a habit with something of this quality, too. It was good that he looked both ways with care. No doubt his scan of the tracks was precise and sensitive. He certainly would have detected any oncoming train. The difficulty was that his habit included a bug, rather like a bug in a computer program. Although his habit had a thoughtful phase (scanning the tracks), he was not thoughtful about his habit (choosing the point where he should scan the tracks).

Thus, the idea of habits of mind is not self-contradictory. A behavior can be habitual in its management but mindful in what it does. Still, one might ask, "Why not have it all? Ideally, shouldn't thinking processes be mindfully managed, mindful through and through for that extra edge?" Probably not! At least three things are wrong with this intuitively appealing ideal.

First, having to manage a thinking process mindfully would likely reduce the thoughtfulness of the process itself. As Herbert Simon (1957) and many other psychologists have emphasized, we humans have a limited capacity for processing information. Committing the management of a thinking process to routine is one way to open up mental space for the work the process has to do. Second, life has many distractions and preoccupations. A well-developed habit is more likely to make its presence felt than a practice that always must be deployed with meticulous deliberateness.

The third objection to this ideal of thoroughly mindful thinking goes beyond these pragmatic considerations to a logical point. Suppose the general rule is that thinking processes need mindful management. Surely managing a thinking process is itself a thinking process, so that process, too, needs mindful management. And the process of managing needs mindful management, and so on. It is mindful management all the way up, an infinite tower of metacognition, each process managed by its own mindfully managed manager. Clearly this approach won't work. Enter habits of mind, an apt challenge to a misguided conception of thinking as thoroughly thoughtful.

The notion of habits of mind also challenges another conception: the notion of intelligence. Most of the research on human intelligence is emphatically "abilities centric" (Perkins, Jay, & Tishman, 1993; Perkins, 1995). As mentioned in Chapter 1 of Book 1, the IQ tradition sees intelligence as a pervasive, monolithic mental ability, summed up by IQ and Charles Spearman's (1904) "g" factor, a statistical construct representing general intelligence. A number of theorists have proposed that there are many kinds of mental ability (two to 150, according to one model developed by Guilford [1967]). Although this book is not a setting where these models bear review (see Perkins, 1995), most of these models have something in common: They treat intelligence as an "ability on demand." Intelligence becomes a matter of what you can do when you know what it is that you're supposed to try to do (such as complete this analogy, decide whether this inference is warranted, or find the best definition for this word).

Thinking in much of life is a different matter. In daily life, we not only have to solve problems, we also have to find them amid an ongoing, complex stream of stimuli imposing constant demands and distractions. On the road of life, our thinking is not just a matter of the thinking we can do when we know a peak performance is demanded. It also is a matter of our sensitivity to occasions and our inclination to invest ourselves in them thoughtfully. High mental ability alone may serve us well when we're sitting at a desk, our pencils poised, but good habits of mind keep us going in the rest of the world. This point is underscored by scholars such as philosopher Robert Ennis (1986), with his analysis of critical thinking dispositions; psychologist Jonathan Baron (1985), with his dispositional model of intelligence; and psychologist Ellen Langer (1989), with her conception of mindfulness.

A program of empirical research on thinking dispositions, which my colleague Shari Tishman and I have directed over the past several years, underscores what's at stake here (e.g., Perkins & Tishman, 1997). Working with students from middle to late elementary school, we investigated their performance on a variety of critical and creative thinking tasks involving narratives. Over and over again, we found that they could do far better than they did do when they explored options, considered pros and cons, and performed similar tasks. Their performance was limited because they often did not detect when such moves were called for. When they did detect what they should do, or when the places were pointed out, they easily could show the kind of thinking called for. They didn't lack intelligence in the sense of ability on demand, but they lacked the habits of mind that provide for ongoing alertness to shortfalls in thinking.

In that spirit, this series of four books speaks not just to intelligence in the laboratory but also to intelligent behavior in the real world. It addresses how we can help youngsters get ready for the road of life, a sort of "drivers' education" for the mind. Imagine what life would be like without good habits of various sorts. Our teeth would rot, our bodies collapse, our gardens wither, our tempers sour, and our friends drift away. We do better to the extent that we get direction from good habits, including habits of mind. When today's students hit the road, the ideas in Habits of Mind: A Developmental Series can help them ride on smooth mental wheels, checking for trains *before* they start over the tracks!

REFERENCES

Baron, J. (1985). *Rationality and intelligence.* New York: Cambridge University Press.

Dewey, J. (1933). *How we think: A restatement of the relation of reflective thinking to the education process.* New York: D. C. Heath.

Ennis, R. H. (1986). A taxonomy of critical thinking dispositions and abilities. In J. B. Baron & R. S. Sternberg (Eds.), *Teaching thinking skills: Theory and practice* (pp. 9–26). New York: W. H. Freeman.

Guilford, J. P. (1967). *The nature of human intelligence.* New York: McGraw-Hill.

Langer, E. J. (1989). *Mindfulness.* Reading, MA: Addison-Wesley.

Perkins, D. N. (1995). *Outsmarting IQ: The emerging science of learnable intelligence.* New York: The Free Press.

Perkins, D. N., Jay, E., & Tishman, S. (1993). Beyond abilities: A dispositional theory of thinking. *The Merrill-Palmer Quarterly, 39*(1), 1–21.

Perkins, D. N., & Tishman, S. (1997). *Dispositional aspects of intelligence.* Paper presented at the Second Spearman Seminar, The University of Plymouth, Devon, England.

Simon, H. A. (1957). *Models of man: Social and rational.* New York: Wiley.

Spearman, C. (1904). General intelligence, objectively defined and measured. *American Journal of Psychology, 15*, 201–209.

PREFACE TO THE SERIES

ARTHUR L. COSTA AND BENA KALLICK

D onna Norton Swindal, a resource teacher in Burnsville, Minnesota, recently shared an interesting story about a 4th grader who brought a newspaper clipping to class. The article described genocide in a troubled African country. After a lively discussion about what was happening there, one concerned classmate stated, "If those people would just learn to persist, they could solve their problems."

His philosophical colleague added, "If they would learn to listen with understanding and empathy, they wouldn't have this problem."

Yet another activist suggested, "We need to go over there and teach them the habits of mind!"

What are the "habits of mind" these concerned young citizens were so eager to share? They are the overarching theme of Habits of Mind: A Developmental Series, and they are the heart of the book you now hold in your hands.

THE BEGINNING

The ideas in Habits of Mind: A Developmental Series first started in 1982. Our beginning conversations about Intelligent Behaviors flourished into rich experiments with classroom practitioners until finally we arrived at this juncture: a series of four books to inspire the work of others. In our daily work with students and staff, we discovered that names were needed for the behaviors that would be expected from one another if, indeed, we were living in a productive learning organization. We came to call these dispositions "habits of mind," indicating that the behaviors require a discipline of the mind that is practiced so it becomes a habitual way of working toward more thoughtful, intelligent action.

The intent of Habits of Mind: A Developmental Series is to help educators teach toward these habits of mind, which we see as broad, enduring, and essential lifespan learnings that are as appropriate for adults as they are for students. Our hope is that by teaching students (and adults) the habits of mind, students will be more disposed to draw upon the habits when they are faced with uncertain or challenging situations. And, ultimately, we hope the habits will help educators develop thoughtful, compassionate, and cooperative human beings who can live productively in an increasingly chaotic, complex, and information-rich world (as the 4th graders above so aptly demonstrated!).

The most powerful communities use these habits of mind to guide all their work. Yet sometimes the practicality of school life requires that people make individual commitments with the hope that their beliefs and behaviors will affect the whole. Teaching with the habits of mind requires a shift toward a broader conception of educational outcomes and how they are cultivated, assessed, and communicated. Taken together, the four books in Habits of Mind: A Developmental Series aim to help you work toward and achieve these goals.

A DUAL PURPOSE

In this four-book series, we provide

- Descriptions and examples of the habits of mind.
- Instructional strategies intended to foster acquisition of these habits at school and at home.
- Assessment tools that provide a means of gathering evidence of student growth in the habits of mind.
- Ways of involving students, teachers, and parents in communicating progress toward acquiring the habits of mind.
- Descriptions from schools, teachers, and administrators about how they have incorporated the habits of mind and the effects of their work.

Our true intent for these books, however, is far more panoramic, pervasive, and long-range. Each book in the series works at two levels. The first level encompasses immediate and practical considerations that promote using the habits of mind in classrooms and schools every day. The second level addresses a larger, more elevated concern for creating a learning culture that considers habits of mind as central to building a thoughtful community. We summarize these levels as follows.

BOOK 1: *DISCOVERING AND EXPLORING HABITS OF MIND*

Level 1: Defining the habits of mind and understanding the significance of developing these habits as a part of lifelong learning.

Level 2: Encouraging schools and communities to elevate their level and broaden their scope of curricular outcomes by focusing on more essential, enduring lifespan learnings.

BOOK 2: *ACTIVATING AND ENGAGING HABITS OF MIND*

Level 1: Learning how to teach the habits directly and to reinforce them throughout the curriculum.

Level 2: Enhancing instructional decision making to employ content not as an end of instruction but as a vehicle for activating and engaging the mind.

BOOK 3: *ASSESSING AND REPORTING ON HABITS OF MIND*

Level 1: Learning about a range of techniques and strategies for gathering evidence of students' growth in and performance of the habits of mind.

Level 2: Using feedback to guide students to become self-assessing and to help school teams and parents use assessment data to cultivate a more thoughtful culture.

BOOK 4: *INTEGRATING AND SUSTAINING HABITS OF MIND*

Level 1: Learning strategies for extending the impact of habits of mind throughout the school community.

Level 2: Forging a common vision among all members of the educational community from kindergarten through post-graduate work: teachers, administrative teams, administrators, librarians, staff developers, teacher educators, school board members, and parents. This vision describes the characteristics of efficacious and creative thinkers and problem solvers.

In teaching for the habits of mind, we are interested in not only how many answers students know but also how students behave when they don't know an answer. We are interested in observing how students produce knowledge rather than how they merely reproduce it. A critical attribute of intelligent human beings is not only having information but also knowing how to act on it.

By definition, a problem is any stimulus, question, task, phenomenon, or discrepancy, the explanation for which is not immediately known. Intelligent behavior is performed in response to such questions and problems. Thus, we are interested in focusing on student performance under those challenging conditions—dichotomies, dilemmas, paradoxes, ambiguities and enigmas—that demand strategic reasoning, insightfulness, perseverance, creativity and craftsmanship to resolve them.

Teaching toward the habits of mind is a team effort. Because repeated opportunities over a long period are needed to acquire these habits of mind, the entire staff must dedicate itself to teaching toward, recognizing, reinforcing, discussing, reflecting on, and assessing the habits of mind. When students encounter these habits at each grade level in the elementary years and in each classroom throughout the secondary day—and when the habits also are reinforced and modeled at home—they become internalized, generalized, and habituated.

We need to find new ways of assessing and reporting growth in the habits of mind. We cannot measure process-oriented outcomes using old-fashioned, product-oriented assessment techniques. Gathering evidence of performance and growth in the habits of mind requires "kid watching." As students interact with real-life, day-to-day problems in school, at home, on the playground, alone, and with friends, teaching teams and other adults can collect anecdotes and examples of written and visual expressions that reveal students' increasingly voluntary and spontaneous use of these habits of mind. This work also takes time. The habits are never fully mastered, though they do become increasingly apparent over time and with repeated experiences and opportunities to practice and reflect on their performance.

Considered individually, each book helps you start down a path that will lead to enhanced curriculum, instruction, and assessment practices. Taken together, the books in Habits of Mind: A Developmental Series provide a road map for individuals, for classrooms, and ultimately for a full-system approach. For our purposes, we think a "system" is approached when the habits of mind are integrated throughout the culture of the organization. That is, when all individual members of a learning community share a common vision of the attributes of effective and creative problem solvers, when resources are allocated to the development of those dispositions; when strategies to enhance those characteristics in themselves and others are planned, and when members of the organization join in efforts to continuously assess, refine, and integrate those behaviors in their own and the organization's practices.

> I can tell you right now that we will never be able to forget the
> habits of mind. They helped us so much! They taught us better

ways of doing things and how to resolve problems! We learned respect and manners. My mother was so very impressed with this teaching. Also we learned that you need to get along with others and not to disrespect them either.

Excerpted from a 5th grader's
valedictorian address upon graduation from
Friendship Valley Elementary School, Westminster, Maryland

PREFACE TO BOOK 2

ARTHUR L. COSTA AND BENA KALLICK

This second book of Habits of Mind: A Developmental Series aims to help you translate the habits of mind into action. Chapter 1 describes the first step in this process: creating school and classroom conditions that signal "thoughtful" behavior. It is unlikely that students will acquire the habits of mind unless the school, home, and classroom environments signal trust, warmth, and risk taking. This chapter describes a variety of elements that promote those conditions. The chapter also considers five specific response behaviors that foster students' acquisition of the habits of mind: silence, providing data, accepting without judgment, clarifying, and empathizing.

Chapter 2 considers how to use linguistic tools to purposely enhance awareness and use of the habits of mind. The chapter opens with a "word splash," which is a strategy for developing fluency and flexibility in recognizing and communicating about the habits of mind. You need not always use the exact terminology of the habits of mind as we describe them. For example, we know that if people use phrases such as "stick to it," "hang in there," or "don't give up," they are talking about the habit of mind we generally call "persisting." Still, because language is the major medium of instruction and communication, great care must be taken to consciously and deliberately use language that evokes, labels, and models the habits of mind. The remainder of this chapter considers strategies for achieving those goals.

Because the habits of mind are performed in response to problems, the answers to which are not immediately known, Chapter 3 explores teacher-questioning strategies. Questioning strategies are a rich opportunity for developing student engagement and drawing children into the learning process.

David Hyerle, an expert in the use of thinking maps, contributes Chapter 4. He synthesizes the use of visual tools to help students become more aware of the habits of mind through their visual representations.

Chapter 5 explores how teachers can infuse the habits of mind into their lesson planning. This chapter provides a variety of suggestions for designing units, lessons, and learning tasks centered around the habits of mind.

Chapter 6 offers a collection of practical suggestions for teaching each of the 16 habits of mind directly. We encourage you to continually add to this material and share ideas with colleagues. We suggest developing files of "lesson banks" about the habits of mind, which can be shared and expanded. For example, the CD-ROM *Tech Paths for Math* follows a common template for unit design that all teachers can use (Kallick & Wilson, 1998). This provides a structured source of information about units that can be organized into a database for teachers to retrieve and use.

We often are asked about the relationship between the content teachers are responsible for teaching and the habits of mind. Chapters 7–13, contributed by a variety of practitioners, address these relationships.

Rest assured, we still want students to learn to read, to compute, to understand principles of science, and to become literate. For our purposes, however, these subject areas are not ends but means. They are the vehicles for carrying out and practicing the habits of mind. Whether you are a successful scientist, mathematician, artist, or athlete, you still need general dispositions such as persistence, creativity, and striving for accuracy.

Chapters 7–13 contain contributions from teachers in commonly taught school subjects: literature, math, music, foreign language, reading, character education, and social science. Each chapter highlights opportunities for practicing and applying one or more habits of mind. Not all school subjects are visited. However, this broad representation provides real-life illustrations of how the habits of mind are relevant in all grades throughout the curriculum. Chapter 14 offers suggestions for getting started implementing the habits of mind in your school and classroom.

This book provides a wealth of suggestions for teaching the habits of mind directly as well as strategies for infusing them throughout curriculum and instruction. These are not prescriptions or recipes, however. We hope they stimulate your creativity and help you get started. In our experience, once teachers work with the habits and observe positive results in students, they begin to look for more ways to integrate them into the work of the classroom and the school. Soon, everyone is in the habit of using the habits of mind!

REFERENCE

Kallick, B., & Wilson, J. (1998). *Tech paths for math* [CD-ROM]. Guilford, CT: Technology Pathways.

From the Editors: Throughout the book, student names are fictitious.

1

CREATING "THOUGHTFUL" CLASSROOM ENVIRONMENTS

ARTHUR L. COSTA AND BENA KALLICK

I am looking at a behavior called persistence. It means like people that never give up. For an example, Christopher Columbus sailed to the Indies to look for gold. He kept on going back to the Indies to search for gold. He never found it. But the thing he did, he never gave up looking for it. That's what persistence means.

And another book I read is Katy and the Big Snow. *One day it was snowing bad and the snow was about 18 inches tall. The whole town couldn't get out of their houses because the snow was covering it. When Katy saw all the snow she decided to take all the snow out. It took her one day to clean up the snow. She didn't sleep. She didn't even get tired. She never stopped taking out all the snow. I learned that people who never give up are very brave.*

Student at Hidden Valley Elementary School
Burnsville, Minnesota

We begin this second book in Habits of Mind: A Developmental Series by considering classrooms and schools where the habits of mind already flourish. How have these educators created thoughtful environments where students encounter, think about, and develop habits of mind? Specifically, how have teachers created environments where children discover the habits of mind in the characters of a novel or describe them through the heroes of history? How have teachers helped children gain insight about their own habits of mind based on what they've learned from others? Exactly what characterizes these kinds of rich learning environments?

A DEEPLY HELD BELIEF

In classrooms where the habits of mind succeed, we find a deeply held belief that all students can continue to develop and improve. For many years, educators and parents alike believed that thinking skills programs were intended to challenge the intellectually gifted. Indeed, some thought that any child whose IQ fell below a certain score was doomed to remedial work or compensatory drill-and-practice. Much research, however, with hydrocephalic, Down syndrome, senile, and brain-damaged persons demonstrates that almost anyone can achieve amazing growth in intelligent behavior with proper intervention (Feuerstein, Feuerstein, & Schur, 1997).

In classrooms where the habits of mind succeed, we also find a belief that the habits of mind aren't just "kid stuff." Teachers, parents, and administrators can also monitor and modify their own habits of mind, such as managing impulsivity, thinking about thinking (metacognition), listening with understanding and empathy, and thinking flexibly. We never fully master the habits of mind. Though we begin work with the habits as children, we continue to develop and improve them throughout our lives.

HABITS OF MIND AS GOALS

Students often expend great amounts of energy trying to figure out a teacher's intentions. In classrooms where the habits of mind succeed, teachers make one intention explicit: Mastering the habits of mind is the goal of students' education. They also help students see that the responsibility for thinking is theirs.

Students grasp that mastering the habits of mind is a classroom goal when thinking becomes the content. They come to understand that having more than one solution to a problem is desirable. They see that it is commendable when they take time to plan for and reflect on an answer rather than respond impulsively. They also learn that it is desirable to change an answer with additional information.

IT TAKES TIME

In most schools, educational innovations are seldom institutionalized: "Last year we did performance standards, and the year before it was mission statements." Many educators believe the "thinking movement" has been succeeded by the "authentic assessment" movement, not realizing that thinking is central to the authentic practices they now pursue so fervently. Experience tells us it takes about three to four years of well-defined instruction with qualified teachers and carefully constructed curriculum materials for the habits of mind to "succeed." After three or four years in a school, we've started to observe significant and enduring changes in students' behavior.

If students are to "habituate" the habits of mind, they must encounter them again and again throughout the elementary and secondary years in every subject and in every classroom. Educators must teach the habits of mind and thinking skills directly. We know that the amount of time on task affects students' academic learning. This relationship also is true for acquiring thinking skills. When thinking becomes a goal of instruction, teachers and administrators place greater value on learning activities that stimulate cognitive processes.

Time is also an issue because some students come from homes, classrooms, or schools where the habits of mind are not valued. These children can be dismayed by and resistant to a teacher's invitations to use the habits. Time and consistent instruction are necessary to overcome this reluctance.

A RICH, RESPONSIVE ENVIRONMENT

Students must work in a rich, responsive environment if they are to make the habits of mind their own. They need access to a variety of resources that they can manipulate, experience, and observe. For example, the classroom should be filled with a variety of data sources: books, encyclopedias, almanacs, videos, CD-ROMs, and databases. Do students have contact with knowledgeable people in the community? Or can they contact others through the Internet to explore theories and test ideas? Field trips are important, too, not just for their content but because they provide students opportunities to plan for and reflect on learning.

Thanks to technology, the world beyond the school isn't as far away as it once was. Students manage more information and resources than ever before. As they move into adulthood, they will need the discipline of the habits of mind to guide their higher education and their careers. A rich, responsive classroom environment helps prepare them for all these experiences.

ATTENTION TO READINESS AND SEQUENCE

Both the nature of thinking capabilities and the sequence in which they appear have been well established in human beings. Too often, however, educators disregard these theories and present learning activities before students are ready for them developmentally. To find success, educators must introduce curriculum for the habits of mind in a sequence that matches children's development.

One of the chief causes for failure in formal education is that educators begin with abstractions through print and language rather than with real, material action. Learning progresses through stages of increasing complexity (the number of ideas and factors we can think about) and increasing abstraction (progressing from a concrete object to a pictorial representation of the object to a symbol that stands for the object, to a spoken word that stands for the symbol). Curriculum and instruction—including work with the habits of mind—are more meaningful if they are sequenced in a manner consistent with the stages of cognitive development (Lowery, 1991).

KEEPING TRACK OF LEARNING

In schools where the habits of mind are a success, students keep track of their learning. Children write about, illustrate, and reflect on the use of the habits of mind in a personal log or diary. This work allows them to synthesize their thoughts and actions and to translate them into symbolic form. Reflection helps students truly make the habits of mind their own.

A log or diary also provides students the opportunity to revisit their initial perceptions about the habits of mind. Then they can compare any changes in those perceptions. Students also can chart the processes of strategic thinking and decision making, identifying "blind alleys" and recalling successes and "tragedies" of experimentation. For a variation on written journals, consider making videotape or audiotape recordings of projects and performances.

CLASSROOM DISCUSSIONS

Guided discussions are always a useful way for teachers to offer insight about the habits of mind. Discussions also provide an opportunity for students to process their learning.

Talking about situations in which habits of mind were, are, or could be applied is enormously helpful as students learn more and more about the habits. Teachers can guide specific discussions of students' problem-solving processes, inviting them to share their metacognition, reveal their intentions, and examine plans for solving a problem.

FREQUENT INFUSION OF THE HABITS

Teachers who are successful with the habits of mind use every possible opportunity to teach the habits. They are always on the lookout for occasions where the habits of mind would be useful to solve a problem, resolve a conflict, or make a decision.

Have students noticed the habits of mind (or lack thereof) in their favorite television shows? Can they find them in the literature they're reading for English class? Are the habits of mind evident in news events? Occasionally it's useful to set up simulations that require using the habits of mind. Such activities reinforce the concept that students always must be ready to call on these dispositions.

The habits of mind are most evident when we ask students to manage their own learning. Consider all the different habits of mind involved when we ask students to choose the group they will join, the topic they will study, and the ways that they will manage themselves to meet a deadline. Every occasion of self-directed learning is a rich opportunity for students to practice the habits of mind.

A "THOUGHTFUL" ENVIRONMENT

When we say the classroom must be a thoughtful environment, we are playing on the meaning for the word *thoughtful:* (1) to be "full of thought" and (2) to be caring and sensitive, to be "thoughtful" of others. The manner in which teachers and administrators respond to students can create and sustain a thoughtful environment that creates trust; allows risk taking; and is experimental, creative, and positive. This environment requires listening to each other's ideas, remaining nonjudgmental, and having rich data sources. Lisa Davis of West Orchard Elementary School in Chappaqua, New York, describes her experiences with a thoughtful environment this way:

Habits of mind are a natural part of my classroom community because they are the attributes that my students and I strive to embrace as learners on a daily basis. Early in my career, I knew that I didn't want to respond to my students by saying, "Good answer," or "Great work." I didn't want to use those comments because they have little meaning, except to imply that the child's answer *prior* to the "great one" wasn't as good. Or, it tells the child who might have answered next to give up because the "great answer" already has been given.

Taking my cues from an art education course, I knew that if I could be specific in my praise it would have a more meaningful effect. For example, if you say to a child, "That's a great painting," the child might temporarily feel good about the praise. If you say, however, "I like the way you mixed the colors blue, white, and green in the ocean. It gives me a feeling of movement," the child is required to engage and reflect on the comment. Even if she disagrees, she is still engaged in a thought process that, more than likely, will trigger the idea of "movement" the next time she attempts a similar task.

Evaluative comments tend to shut down thinking, and "thin comments," as my 4th graders refer to them, don't give the learner any information. My question, then, became, "How can I respond with 'thick,' or meaningful, praise in the classroom without being evaluative?" The habits of mind helped me be specific in my praise by making me focus on what's important. While the right answer is a "good" thing to strive for, it's really the process one goes through to get the right answer that interests me.

In my own teaching, I've tried to get away from saying, "good answer" or "right." Instead, I try to note when a child is using an intelligent behavior. It's like saying "Nice job!" to a child who is painting, instead of being specific and saying, "I like the choice of color here; it gives me a warm feeling." My comments are much more meaningful, but better than that is seeing kids recognize their peers. I have often found that the child that might be slower in completing work or has a difficult time grasping new concepts is thought to be not as smart by his or her peers. Now students hear me say, "[Kenny], you are a persistent problem solver." [Kenny] is being rewarded for his persistence, not just his answer.

Successful teachers like Lisa Davis use the following five kinds of response behaviors to create an atmosphere in which students experience and practice the habits of mind: silence, providing data, accepting without judgment, clarifying, and empathizing.

SILENCE

In some schools, teachers dominate classroom talk with a rapid-fire pace and lower-level cognitive questions. A teacher may wait less than one second after posing a question before doing one of several things: repeating the question, commenting on a student answer, redirecting the question to a new student, answering the question, or starting a new questioning sequence.

In these kinds of exchanges, student answers are often terse or fragmentary, or the student's tone of voice shows a lack of confidence. After a student replies, the teacher may wait less than one second before commenting or asking another question. Students have little chance for second thoughts or to extend their ideas. Many teachers appear programmed to accept only one, predetermined, "right" answer. They leave little room for alternate answers or differing opinions. Students receive the message that "the teacher's way of knowing is the *only* way of knowing."

Silence, or wait time, is one answer to this situation. Mary Budd Rowe first explored the concept of wait time in the late 1960s (Rowe 1969, 1974). During classroom observations, she noticed that some teachers used "purposeful pauses" as they conducted lessons and class discussions. In these classrooms, she noted students making speculations, holding sustained conversational sequences, posing alternative explanations, and arguing over the interpretation of data. She also noted positive changes in the affective climate and the quality of classroom interactions. She observed an increase in the level of cognitive functioning and academic achievement and a decrease in the number of behavior problems. Additional research has shown many positive changes in classrooms where the teacher uses increased wait time:

- The length of student responses increases 300 to 700 percent.
- The number of unsolicited but appropriate student responses increases.
- Failures to respond decrease.
- Student confidence increases, and there are fewer inflected responses.
- Speculative responses increase.
- Student-to-student interaction increases. Teacher-centered show-and-tell decreases.
- Teacher questions change in number and kind: The number of divergent questions increase, and teachers ask higher-level questions (as described by Bloom's taxonomy [1956]). Teachers probe more for clarification.

- Students make inferences and support them with data.
- Students ask more questions.

"Wait Time I" is the length of time a teacher pauses after asking a question. "Wait Time II" is the length of time a teacher waits after a student replies or asks another question. A minimum three-second pause is recommended. With higher-level cognitive tasks, five seconds or more of wait time may be required to achieve positive results. "Wait Time III" is pausing and modeling thoughtfulness after the student asks the teacher a question.

When teachers specifically attend to the habit of mind of questioning and posing problems, they must also attend to wait time. Students need time to be able to think flexibly or creatively. Using longer pauses in group discussions provides students with the necessary think time to help them manage their impulsivity and take responsible risks as they answer questions posed either by the teacher or by the work they are studying.

Rowe also examined the use of longer pauses in whole-group lecture settings. Students need mental processing time in information-dense subjects like chemistry, physics, and geology. Her research indicates that retention and understanding increase when students are provided with 2 to 3 minutes for discussion, clarifying notes, and raising questions after every 8 to 10 minutes of instruction. (All unresolved student questions should be reserved for the last five minutes of the class period.)

Providing Data

One purpose for cultivating the habits of mind is to guide learners to process data by comparing, classifying, making inferences, or drawing causal relationships for themselves. They must have data to process. Providing data means that the teacher actually supplies data or the teacher helps students acquire the information on their own. The teacher therefore creates a climate that is responsive to the student's quest for information. Teachers can create this climate in several different ways:

1. Sometimes they provide feedback about a student's performance:
   - "No, three times six is not twenty-four. Three times eight is twenty-four."
   - "Yes, you have spelled 'rhythm' correctly."

2. Sometimes they provide personal information, often in the form of "I" messages:
   - "I want you to know that chewing gum in this classroom really disturbs me."

- "John, your pencil tapping is distracting me."
- "The way you painted the tree makes me feel like I'm on the inside looking out."

3. Sometimes teachers make it possible for students to experiment with equipment and materials to find data or information for themselves:
- "Here's a larger test tube if you'd like to see how your experiment would turn out differently."
- "We can see the film again if you want to check your observations."

4. At other times, teachers make primary and secondary sources of information accessible:
- "Mary, this almanac gives information you will need for your report on the world's highest mountain ranges."
- "Here's the dictionary. The best way to verify the spelling is to look it up."

5. Teachers also respond to student requests for information. When a student asks, "What's this thing called?" the teacher replies, "This piece of equipment is called a bell jar."

6. During some exchanges, the teacher surveys the group for students' feelings or to gather information:
- "On this chart we have made a list of what you observed in the film. We can keep this chart in front of us so that we can refer to it as we classify our observations."
- "Let's go around the circle and share some of the feelings we had when we found out the school board decided to close our school."

7. On some occasions, the teacher labels a thinking process or behavior:
- "That is a hypothesis you are posing, Gina."
- "Sharing your crayons like that is an example of cooperation, Mark."
- "Xavier, the question you are asking is an attempt to verify the data."

ACCEPTING WITHOUT JUDGMENT

Nonjudgmental teachers accept what students say and do. When they accept, they give no clues through posture, gesture, or word whether a student's idea, behavior, or feeling is good, bad, better, worse, right, or wrong. Mother Teresa summarized this concept quite simply: "If you judge people, you have no time to love them."

Acceptance of students' ideas or actions provides a psychologically safe climate where children can take risks, make decisions for themselves, and explore the consequences of their actions. Acceptance provides conditions where students are encouraged to examine and compare their own data, values, ideas, criteria, and feelings with others' as well as the teacher's. Although a teacher may offer acceptance in many different ways, we would like to consider two types of nonjudgmental, accepting responses: acknowledgment and paraphrasing.

An acknowledgment simply communicates that a student's ideas have been heard. These are passive responses because the teacher merely conveys that an answer was heard, not necessarily that it was understood.

Examples of passive, nonverbal acknowledgments are nodding the head or recording without change a student's statement on the chalkboard. Here are examples of passive, verbal acknowledgments:

- "Um-hmm."
- "Let's add that as a possibility."
- "Thank you. I'll add your suggestion to our list."
- "I think I understand your explanation."

A second specific form of accepting without judgment is paraphrasing, which can be defined as responding to what the student says or does by rephrasing, recasting, translating, or summarizing. Teachers use this response when they want to extend, build upon, synthesize, or give an example based on the student's answer. Though the teacher may use words that are different from those of the student, the teacher strives to maintain the intent and accurate meaning of the student's idea. This is an active kind of acceptance because the teacher demonstrates that the student's message was received *and* understood. Here are examples of paraphrasing:

- "Your explanation is that if the heat were increased, the molecules would move faster and therefore disperse the food coloring faster."
- "I understand. Your idea is that we should all write our legislators rather than send them one letter from the group."
- "Shaun's idea is that the leaves could be classified according to their shapes, while Sarah's way is to group them by size."
- "An example of what you mean was when we arranged our rock collection according to several different classification systems."

At this point, it's also important to consider briefly the use of praise and rewards in the classroom. In all conversations with students, keep in mind that praise and rewards can be counterproductive if motivation already is evident when a student is engaged in desired behaviors. Praise uses positive value judgments such as good, excellent, and great. Additional praise actually can reduce enthusiasm rather than reinforce it and increase motivation. Unfortunately, many students lack motivation, and some teachers use rewards to try and instill motivation. Rewards, however, are not the entire answer, either.

Joyce and Showers (1988) state: "Praise and rewards, which are often associated with moderate class mean gains, were negatively correlated with both high and low achievers" (p. 56). Using rewards and praise to motivate student learning increases the students' dependency on others for learning. They don't come to find the learning inherently satisfying, and they don't come to value the acquisition or exercise of skills (Lepper & Green, 1978; Kohn, 1994; Deci, 1995). Praise builds conformity, and it makes students dependent on others for their worth. Praise also has been found to be a detriment to creativity (Amabile, 1979).

Although we acknowledge some of the problems with praise, we do not suggest that you eliminate praise altogether. Praise is entirely appropriate at some times and can be used judiciously. For example, praise might be appropriate when students have obeyed rules or changed behaviors to the benefit of themselves and the class. Or, praise can be useful in developmentally appropriate instances with young children. Praising seems best used with certain students and for certain tasks.

If you offer praise, it is important to describe the criteria for the praise. What makes an act "good" or "excellent" must be communicated along with the praise. This way, students understand the reason or criteria that makes the act acceptable, and they can repeat the performance.

Most teachers enjoy rewarding and praising their students. Brophy (1981), however, found that the one person in the classroom for whom praise has the most beneficial effect is the teacher. It is understandable, therefore, that research studies showing the detrimental effects of rewards are met with resistance.

CLARIFYING

Clarifying is similar to accepting without judgment; both behaviors reflect the teacher's concern for fully understanding the student's idea. Accepting without judgment, however, can demonstrate that the teacher understands. Clarifying means the teacher does not understand what the student says and needs more information.

If a student uses unusual terminology, expresses a confused concept or idea, or asks a question that the teacher does not understand, the teacher will want to clarify both the content of that idea and possibly the process by which that idea was derived. The teacher may express a lack of understanding of the student's idea and seek further explanation; invite the student to be more specific by requesting that the student elaborate on or rephrase the idea; or seek to discover the thinking processes underlying the production of that idea.

The intent of clarifying is to better understand the student's ideas, feelings, and thought processes. Clarifying is not a way to change or redirect what the student thinks or feels. Do not use clarifying as a way to direct students' attention to the "correct answer." Clarifying is often stated in the form of an interrogative, but it also could be a statement inviting further illumination. Here are examples:

- "Could you explain to us what you mean by *charisma*?"
- "What you are saying is that you'd rather work by yourself than in a group. Is that correct?"
- "Go over that one more time, Shelley. I'm not sure I understand you."
- "You say you are studying the situation. Tell us just exactly what you do when you 'study' something."
- "Explain to us the steps you took to arrive at that answer."

By clarifying, teachers show students that their ideas are worthy of exploration and consideration. Clarifying demonstrates that the teacher is interested in, values, and wants to pursue students' thinking. When a teacher responds to students' comments by encouraging them to elaborate further, students become more purposeful in their thinking and behaving.

EMPATHIZING

Empathizing is a response that acknowledges cognition *and* accepts feelings. Teachers respond this way when they especially want to recognize a student's feelings, emotions, or behaviors. Often, teachers show empathy when they share similar feelings from their own experiences. This response communicates that the teacher hears not only the student's idea but also the emotions underlying it.

Empathic acceptance can be important because many students come to school from dysfunctional, impoverished environments. The emotions and feelings they bring to school affect their learning and motivation.

Empathic acceptance does not mean a teacher condones acts of aggression or destructive behavior. Empathic acceptance simply means the teacher acknowledges both emotion and cognition. Some examples of empathic acceptance are

- "I can see why you're confused. Those directions are unclear to me, too."
- "You're frustrated because you didn't get a chance to share your idea. We've all got to take turns, and that requires patience. It's hard to wait when you're anxious to share."
- [A student enters the room and slams a workbook on a desk.] "Something must be upsetting you today. Did you have difficulty with that assignment?"

As shown in Figure 1.1, we use the acronym "SPACE" to help remember all these behaviors that help create a thoughtful environment. This acronym—and the behaviors it represents—can be taught to students, parents, or anyone involved in schools and school improvement.

FIGURE 1.1
Gimme "SPACE"!

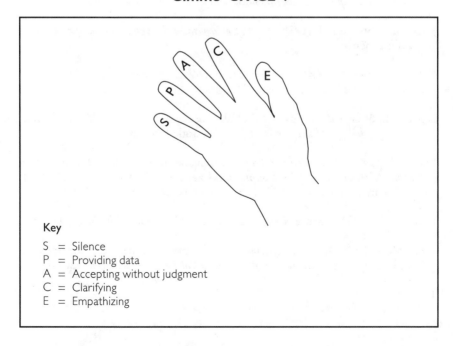

Key

S = Silence
P = Providing data
A = Accepting without judgment
C = Clarifying
E = Empathizing

"SPACE" represents a set of behaviors that start you on your way to successful use of the habits of mind. These behaviors—silence, providing data, accepting without judgment, clarifying, and empathizing—are important for students beginning to learn the habits of mind. By using these behaviors, teachers can begin to build an environment in which the habits of mind flourish.

REFERENCES

Amabile, T. (1979). Effects of external evaluation on artistic creativity. *Journal of Personality and Social Psychology 37*(2), 221–233.

Bloom, B. (Ed.). (1956). *Taxonomy of educational objectives: Classification of educational goals.* New York: Longman, Green and Co.

Brophy, J. E. (1981, October). *Teacher praise: A functional analysis* [Occasional Paper No. 28]. East Lansing, MI: Michigan State University Institute for Research on Teaching.

Deci, E. (1995). *Why we do what we do.* New York: Grosset Putnam.

Feuerstein, R., Feuerstein, R., & Schur, Y. (1997). Process as content in education of exceptional children. In A. Costa & R. Liebmann (Eds.), *Supporting the spirit of learning when process is content.* Thousand Oaks, CA: Corwin Press.

Joyce, B., & Showers, B. (1988). *Student achievement through staff development.* New York: Longman.

Kohn, A. (1994). *Punished by rewards: The trouble with gold stars, incentive plans, A's, praise and other bribes.* New York: Houghton Mifflin.

Lepper, M., & Green, D. (Eds.). (1978). *The hidden cost of rewards: New perspectives on the psychology of human motivation.* New York: Erlbaum.

Lowery, L. (1991). The biological basis for thinking. In A. Costa (Ed.), *Developing minds: A resource book for teaching thinking* (Rev. ed., Vol. 1, pp. 108–117). Alexandria, VA: Association for Supervision and Curriculum Development.

Rowe, M. B. (1969). Science, silence and sanctions. *Science and Children 6*, 11–13.

Rowe, M. B. (1974). Wait time and rewards as instructional variables: Their influence on language, logic and fate control. *Journal of Research in Science Teaching 11*, 81–94.

2

TOWARD A MINDFUL LANGUAGE OF LEARNING

ARTHUR L. COSTA AND BENA KALLICK

Years of research have demonstrated the close, intertwined relationship of language and thought. In fact, the cognitive processes that children derive are embedded in the vocabulary, inflections, and syntax of adults' language. From birth, children imitate the sounds, words, phrases, and thought patterns of the significant adults in their lives (Vygotsky, 1962; Feuerstein, 1980; Flavell, 1977). Through these interactions in their formative years, children develop foundations of thought that endure throughout their lives.

Environments and interactions that demand and provide models of complex language and thought contribute to children's abilities to handle complex thinking processes as they mature (Sternberg & Caruso, 1985). This research concerns us because the past two decades have seen significant transformations in U.S. families. With more working parents, broken homes, and latchkey kids, it is surprising how little time parents and children actually spend talking together. Family life in the United States today often lacks the meaningful verbal interaction necessary to build a foundation for thinking, learning, and communicating in school. When children enter school lacking the complexity of language and thought needed to master academic demands, they often are disadvantaged.

Language is a foundation for the habits of mind. A person must have both inner and expressive language to be able to develop the habits of mind. For example, if students do not have inner language (talking to themselves), they will have difficulty thinking through a problem or being aware of their own thinking so they can use what they have learned in other situations. If a person does not have expressive language (talking to others), they will be unable to participate in social thinking or to articulate questions.

Success in school and daily life depends upon the autonomous application of the habits of mind during problem solving, innovating, and decision making. As adults, we can stimulate, engage, and help children practice the habits of mind by subtly and carefully using language with selected syntax, presuppositions, vocabulary, and intonations.

For example, teachers can consciously select key cognitive terminology so students encounter the words in common, everyday dialogue. We can formulate questions that lead students to exercise certain habits of mind. We can provide data that students must interpret for themselves. We can remain nonjudgmental so children must make their own judgments. In other words, educators can be mindful of their use of language.

We all can develop the habit of thinking and communicating with clarity and precision. In so doing, we educate students' cognitive structures, which ultimately leads to increased academic performance. This chapter contains suggestions for

- Building fluency and a repertoire for the labels of the habits of mind.
- Monitoring our own language.
- Intentionally using language that will enhance awareness and performance of the habits of mind during daily interactions in classrooms and schools.

A "WORD SPLASH"

We begin this chapter with a "word splash," intended to build fluency with the terms and phrases related to each habit of mind. To avoid confusion in this series of books, we tried to use consistently the same terminology each time we named a specific habit of mind. Exact wording is not necessary in the classroom. Clusters of terms have similar meanings for each habit of mind, and the student who can't remember "persisting" may well remember the habit of "stick to it." One way students—and adults—can make these connections is through a word splash.

A word splash is a collection of key terms, synonyms, and phrases that convey meanings similar to a particular term (Lipton & Wellman, 1999). It enhances fluency with the terms and elaborates their meaning. A word splash also enhances flexibility by providing a group of terms rather than restricting someone to use of a single term. A word splash expands the range of questioning and paraphrasing, and it allows students and teachers to communicate with others using common terminology.

Each of the following word splashes was generated by groups of teachers as they considered key terms, synonyms, and word phrases that stand for and convey meanings similar to the terms we use for the habits of mind. To get started, here is a word splash for the phrase "habits of mind":

- Characteristics
- Virtues
- Dispositions
- Qualities
- Attitudes

- Character traits
- Mental disciplines
- Inclinations
- Proclivities

The following sections contain word splashes for each of the 16 habits of mind. These vocabulary lists are by no means complete. You will want to invite your students and colleagues to add to them. For example, students might make a glossary with the habits of mind and then use a thesaurus to add synonyms to their lists. Incorporate these words in your spelling lists, or invite students to go on a scavenger hunt to find additional words and enlarge their mindful vocabulary.

WORD SPLASH FOR PERSISTING

- Never give up
- Perseverance
- Indefatigable
- Focused
- Try and try again
- Stamina
- Continuing
- Stand your ground
- Undaunted
- Drive

- Relentless
- Sustained
- Systematic
- Tenacity
- Diligence
- Reliant
- Enduring
- Stick-to-it-tiveness
- Hang in there
- Hang tough

WORD SPLASH FOR MANAGING IMPULSIVITY

- Think before you act
- Deliberate
- Thoughtful
- Strategic
- Patient
- Meditate
- Self-regulated
- Calm
- Reflective
- Controlled
- Count to 10
- Wait time
- Take a deep breath
- Planned
- Considered

WORD SPLASH FOR LISTENING WITH UNDERSTANDING AND EMPATHY

- Empathic
- Tuned in
- Mirroring
- Attentive
- Attuned
- Caring
- Concentrate
- Paraphrase
- Respectful
- Focused
- Concentration
- Summarizing
- Compassionate

WORD SPLASH FOR THINKING FLEXIBLY

- Adaptable
- Bendable
- Options
- Changing
- Open-minded
- Diversity
- Alternatives
- Expandable
- Plasticity
- Diversity
- Lateral thinking

- Pliable
- Creative
- Different points of view
- Resilient
- Different perspectives
- Growing
- Multiple solutions
- Fluent
- Repertoire
- Many possibilities

WORD SPLASH FOR THINKING ABOUT THINKING (METACOGNITION)

- Self-aware
- Awareness
- Thinking aloud
- Reflective
- Strategic planning
- Have a plan in mind
- Self-evaluative
- Thinking about your thinking
- Knowing what you know
  and what you don't know
- Self-awareness
- Mental maps

- Talking to yourself
- Inner dialogue
- Self-monitoring
- Inside your head
- Inner thoughts
- Inner thoughts
- Inner feelings
- Talk-aloud problem solving
- Consciousness
- Alertness
- Cognizance

WORD SPLASH FOR STRIVING FOR ACCURACY

- Correct
- Craftsmanlike
- Check it out
- Refined
- Adroit
- Hit the bull's-eye
- Sharp
- Perfection
- On target
- Exactness
- Correctness
- Elegant
- Clear
- Specific
- Stamina
- Proof
- Flawless
- Effortless
- Quality
- Surety
- Mastery
- Ensure
- Quality control
- Fit
- Uncompromising
- Zero tolerance
- Finished

WORD SPLASH FOR QUESTIONING AND POSING PROBLEMS

- Interested
- Quest
- Probing
- Clarifying
- Investigative
- Curious
- Interrogative
- Inquisitive
- Skeptical
- Cautious
- Inquiry
- Query
- Seeking
- Proof
- Delving
- Speculative
- Qualify
- Hypothetical
- Investigative
- Curious
- Perplexing

WORD SPLASH FOR APPLYING PAST KNOWLEDGE TO NEW SITUATIONS

- Re-use
- Recycled
- Draw forth
- Know your resources
- Reminds me
- Remember
- Recall
- Apply
- Bridge
- Transfer
- Use again

- Prior knowledge
- Scaffolding
- Just like the time when . . .
- Similar situations
- Reservoir of knowledge/ experiences
- Transform
- Translate
- Implementation
- Utilize

WORD SPLASH FOR THINKING AND COMMUNICATING WITH CLARITY AND PRECISION

- Articulate
- Choice of words
- Grammatically correct
- Communicative
- Enunciate

- Command of the language
- Eloquent
- Define your terms
- Editing

Word Splash for Gathering Data Through All Senses

- Engaged
- Involvement
- Perceptions
- Sensing
- Hands-on
- Interactive
- Touch
- Concrete
- Physical, visual, tactual, kinesthetic
- Feel it
- Experiential
- Perceptual acuity
- Clarity
- Sensitivity
- Move it
- Dance
- Auditory, gustatory, olfactory
- Sensitivities
- Sensations

Word Splash for Creating, Imagining, Innovating

- Unique
- Productive
- Fertile
- Generative
- Brainstorm
- Prolific
- Imaginative
- New
- Fresh
- Ingenious
- Novel
- Fecund
- Fluent
- Engender
- Unconventional
- Inventive
- Clever
- Divergent
- Artistic
- Innovative
- Spontaneous

WORD SPLASH FOR RESPONDING WITH WONDERMENT AND AWE

- Wondrous
- Alive
- Sensation
- Aha!
- Amazed
- Amazement
- Appreciation
- Far out
- Astounding
- Fascination
- Excitement
- Phenomenon
- Awesome
- Passionate
- Marvel
- Exuberant
- Way cool
- Miraculous
- Energized
- Challenged
- Insatiable
- Wide-eyed
- Mysterious
- Visionary
- Obsessed
- Motivated
- Enthralled
- Surprise
- Transfixed

WORD SPLASH FOR TAKING RESPONSIBLE RISKS

- Bold
- Adventuresome
- Courageous
- New pathways
- Exploration
- Daring
- Pathfinders
- Unconventional
- Gamble
- Living on the edge
- Vagabond
- Venture
- Challenged
- Roving
- Individualistic
- Free-spirited
- Do your thing
- Just do it

WORD SPLASH FOR FINDING HUMOR

- Laughable
- Laugh at yourself
- Funny
- Comic
- Comedian
- Absurd
- Bizarre
- Pun
- Jokester
- Irony
- Satirical
- Clown
- Playful
- Caricature
- Fanciful
- Whimsical
- Capricious
- Comedy
- Wittiness
- Funnybone
- Merry disposition

WORD SPLASH FOR THINKING INTERDEPENDENTLY

- Cooperative
- Collegial
- Congenial
- Collaborative
- Sense of community
- Ohana (Hawaiian word for family or team; the spirit of community)
- Family
- Interdependence
- Interconnected
- Support group
- Teamwork
- Reciprocity
- Synergistic
- Mutual
- Harmonious
- Amicable
- Social
- Reciprocal
- Companionship

Word Splash for Remaining Open to Continuous Learning

- Continuous learning
- Problem finding
- Autopoesis
- Insatiable
- Inquisitive
- Self-modifying
- Self-help
- Self-evaluating
- Continual learner

- Lifelong learning
- Perpetual student
- Failing forward
- Learning from experience
- Self-actualizing
- Mastery
- Commitment
- Kaizen
- Dissatisfied

BUILDING "MINDFUL" LANGUAGE

Once you have expanded your language for naming the habits of mind, the next step is to use language tools and strategies intentionally to enhance students' awareness and performance of these intelligent behaviors. Following are several different ways you can encourage the habits through specific, mindful use of language (Costa & Marzano, 1991).

THINKING WORDS

We often hear teachers admonish students to think: "Think hard!" Students sometimes are criticized for not having the inclination to think: "These kids just go off without thinking!" Actually, the term *think* is a vague abstraction covering a wide range of mental activities. Thus, students may not appear to think because

- The vocabulary is a foreign language to them.
- They may not know how to perform the specific skills that the term implies.

When adults speak mindful language, using specific, cognitive terminology and instructing students in ways to perform certain skills, students are more inclined to use those skills (Astington & Olson, 1990). For example,

25

Instead of saying:	Use MINDFUL LANGUAGE by saying:
"Let's look at these two pictures."	"Let's COMPARE these two pictures."
"What do you think will happen when . . . ?"	"What do you PREDICT will happen when . . . ?"
"How can you put those into groups?"	"How can you CLASSIFY . . . ?"
"Let's work this problem."	"Let's ANALYZE this problem."
"What do you think would have happened if . . . ?"	"What do you SPECULATE would have happened if . . . ?"
"What did you think of this story?"	"What CONCLUSIONS can you draw about this story?"
"How can you explain . . . ?"	"What HYPOTHESES do you have that might explain . . . ?"
"How do you know that's true?"	"What EVIDENCE do you have to support . . . ?"
"How else could you use this . . . ?"	"How could you APPLY this . . . ?"

As children hear these cognitive terms in everyday use and experience the cognitive processes that accompany these labels, they internalize the words and use them as part of their own vocabulary. Teachers will also want to give specific instruction in the cognitive functions so that students possess experiential meaning along with the terminology (Beyer, 1991).

COMMUNICATE AND REINFORCE TERMINOLOGY

A 5th grade teacher standing yard duty on the playground noticed the beginnings of a scuffle between two 6th grade boys. She immediately scurried over to break up the fight. Before she got there, however, she overheard one of her 5th graders intervene and say, "Hey, you guys! Restrain your impulsivity!"

Marilyn Tabor
Irvine Unified School District
Irvine, California

Children love to use the habits of mind terminology. Teach them what metacognition, persistence, and impulsivity mean. Ask them to create posters listing the habits of mind. Invite them to create logos and symbols for each habit, and display both the posters and logos on the classroom walls.

When students use one or more of the habits of mind, teachers should be quick to offer a label. The word splash provided earlier in this chapter can help you use a range of labels that have similar meanings. Here are examples of what teachers might say:

- "You really *persisted* on that problem."
- "You *listened* to Danielle and *empathized* with her feelings."
- "I'll give you some more time. I know you are *metacogitating*."
- "That is an intriguing *problem* you are posing."
- "I see that in your *checking* over your story for accuracy, you found some errors needing correction."
- "That problem really *intrigues* you."

DISCIPLINE

When disciplining children, teachers decide which behaviors to discourage and which to reinforce. Disciplining is another opportunity for teachers to speak mindful language and pose questions that cause children to examine their own behavior, search for the consequences of that behavior, and choose more appropriate actions (Bailis & Hunter, 1985). For example,

Instead of saying:	Use MINDFUL LANGUAGE by saying:
"Be quiet!"	"The noise you're making is disturbing us. Is there a way you can work so that we don't hear you?"
"Sarah, get away from Catherine!"	"Sarah, can you find another place to do your best work?"
"Stop interrupting!"	"Since it's Maria's turn to talk, what do you need to do?"
"Stop running!"	"Why do you think we have the rule about always walking in the halls?"

The teacher and other adults must discuss courtesy, appropriate behavior, and classroom and school rules with children if the children are to learn appropriate alternatives. Then, when they forget, they can search their memory for what was learned. Soon they will monitor their own behavior, an important dimension of metacognition (Costa, 1984).

PROVIDE DATA, NOT SOLUTIONS

Sometimes we rob children of the opportunity to take charge of their own behavior by providing solutions, consequences, and appropriate actions for them. If adults would merely provide data as input for children's decision making, they could come to act more autonomously, become aware of the effects of their behavior on others, and become more empathic in sensing others' verbal and nonverbal cues.

We can speak mindful language by giving data, divulging information about ourselves, or sending "I" messages. For example,

When children:	Use MINDFUL LANGUAGE by saying:
Make noise by tapping their pencil	"I want you to know that your pencil tapping is disturbing me."
Interrupt	"I like it when you take turns to speak."
Whine	"It hurts my ears."
Are courteous	"I liked it when you came in so quietly and went right to work."
Chew gum	"I want you to know that gum chewing in my class disturbs me."

Some children, of course, don't recognize these data as cues for self-control. In such cases, you may have to provide more specific directions for appropriate behavior. Start, however, by giving students the chance to control themselves.

CLASSROOM MANAGEMENT

Too often, teachers give all the information so that students merely perform a task without having to infer meaning. Instead, teachers can use mindful language that will lead students to analyze the task, decide on what is needed, and then act autonomously. For example,

Instead of saying:	Use MINDFUL LANGUAGE by saying:
"For our field trip, remember to bring spending money, comfortable shoes, and a warm jacket."	"What must we remember to bring with us on our field trip?"
"The bell has rung; it's time to go home. Clear off your desks, slide your chairs under the desk quietly, and line up at the door."	"The bell has rung. What must we do to get ready to go home?"
"Get 52 cups, 26 scissors, and 78 sheets of paper. Get some butcher paper to cover the desks."	"Everyone will need two paper cups, a pair of scissors, and three sheets of paper. The desktops will need to be protected. Can you figure out what you'll need to do?"
"Remember to write your name in the upper right-hand corner of your paper."	"So that I easily can tell who the paper belongs to, what must you remember to do?"
"You need to start each sentence with a capital and end with a period."	"This sentence would be complete with two additions. Can you figure out what they are?"

METACOGNITION

Thinking about thinking begets more thinking (Costa, 1984). When children describe the mental processes they are using, the data they are lacking, and the plans they are formulating, they think about their own thinking, or metacogitate. When teachers use mindful language, they cause the covert thought processes students experience to become overt. Whimbey refers to this as "Talk Aloud Problem Solving" (Whimbey, 1985). For example,

When students say:	Use MINDFUL LANGUAGE by saying:
"The answer is 43 pounds, 7 ounces."	"Describe the steps you took to arrive at that answer."
"I don't know how to solve this problem."	"What can you do to get started?"
"I'm comparing . . . ."	"What goes on in your head when you compare?"
"I'm ready to begin."	"Describe your plan of action."
"We're memorizing our poems."	"What do you do when you memorize?"
"I like the large one best."	"What criteria are you using to make your choice?"
"I'm finished."	"How do you know you're correct?"

As teachers invite students to describe what's going on inside their heads when thinking takes place, children become more aware of their own thought processes. As they listen to other students describe their metacognitive processes, they develop flexibility of thought and come to appreciate that there are several ways to solve the same problem.

PRESUPPOSITIONS

Language can be interpreted in terms of its "surface" meaning and its "structural" meaning. Surface meaning refers to word definitions, syntax, semantics, grammar, verb forms, and modifiers. Structural meaning refers to the subtle nuances, connotations, feelings, and images the words convey. A presupposition is a hidden, covert, or implicit meaning buried within the structure of the statement or sequence of language. For example, a teacher says, "Even Richard could pass that course." Several meanings are hidden within the substructure of this sentence: That Richard is not too bright a student, and further, that the course must be a cinch! Neither of these pieces of information is overtly present in the surface structure of the sentence. The sentence does not say, "Even Richard, who is not too bright a student, could pass that course, which is a cinch!" The implicit meaning or presupposition, however, is blatant (Elgin, 1980).

Over time, these kinds of messages seep into children's awareness. Usually the children are unaware that such verbal violence is being used against them, but they feel hurt or insulted in response to language that may sound, on the surface, like a compliment. Interestingly, people behave in response to others' perceptions of them: They behave as if they are expected to behave that way. Over time, negative presuppositions accumulate, and they influence students' poor self-esteem and negative self-concepts as thinkers. Negative behavior follows.

Using positive presuppositions is possible. Teachers can purposely select language to convey a positive self-concept as a thinker: "As you plan your project, what criteria for your research report will you keep in mind?" Notice the positive presuppositions: that you are planning, that you know the criteria for the research report, that you can keep them in your mind, and that you can apply them as you work.

Teachers never purposely set out to deprecate a student's self-esteem. These negative presuppositions, however, may creep into the language of classroom interaction. Teachers who speak mindful language monitor their own words to offer positive presuppositions. For example,

Instead of saying:	Use MINDFUL LANGUAGE by saying:
"Why did you forget to do your assignment?"	"As you plan for your assignment, what materials will you need?"
"Why don't you like to paint?"	"We need you to paint a picture to add to our gallery of artists."
"Did you forget again?"	"Tell us what you will do to help you remember."
"When will you grow up?"	"As we grow older, we learn how to solve these problems from such experiences."
"Here, I'll give you an easier puzzle; then you'll be successful."	"As the puzzles get more difficult, how will you use planning like this again?"

STUDYING MINDFUL LANGUAGE

Like any language, mindful language is dynamic. Mindful language can be created, analyzed, refined, and transmitted to others. This language can also became archaic. Students, too, can explore the linguistic structure of mindful language. They can focus on word clusters or syntax cues within the language, which signal what cognitive operations those words evoke. Sometimes this approach is referred to as discourse analysis, which includes such cognitive processes as concept formation, relationship identification, and pattern recognition.

For example, students can search for relationships as a way of linking information. They can find the word or word cluster that cues the thinking process of that relationship. This process is called "relationship identification." Relationship identification requires students to

• Identify separate ideas that are related within a sentence.
• Identify the type of relationship between the ideas: addition, comparison, causality, sequence, or definition.
• Identify the linguistic cues for the performance of that cognitive relationship. Words such as *both, same,* and *similar* indicate comparing. Words such as *however, but,* or *on the other hand* indicate contrasting. Words like *first, next, after,* and *awhile later* indicate sequencing.

Here's another way to look at relationship identification:

Cognitive Process	Type of Relationship	Example of Linguistic Cue
ADDITION	Two ideas go together in the same way.	"He is intelligent AND he is kind."
COMPARISON	Common attributes are shared.	"Shawn AND Sarah BOTH play the violin."
CONTRAST	Two ideas don't go together.	"He is healthy BUT he doesn't exercise."
CAUSALITY	One event causes another.	"Peter went home BECAUSE his work was finished."
SEQUENCE	One event happens before, during, or after another event.	"He went home, THEN he went to the library."

Teaching students to be alert to the cognitive process embedded in written and spoken language can help them become aware of their own language and thought. This instruction also can help them decode the syntactic, semantic, and rhetorical signals found in all languages, and students learn to integrate the complex interaction of language, thought, and action (Marzano & Hutchins, 1985).

Language is a tool for enhancing others' development. Speaking mindful language simply means that we consciously use communication to help students develop the habits of mind. We speak mindful language for a variety of reasons:

1. Using a variety of terms, phrases, and slogans that are synonymous with the habits of mind builds conceptual fluency.

2. Using specific cognitive terminology provides a good model for thinking and communicating with clarity and precision.

3. Posing questions that cause children to examine their own behavior, search for the consequences of that behavior, and choose more appropriate actions serves as a rich model for questioning and posing problems as well as problem solving.

4. Giving data, divulging information about ourselves, or sending "I" messages so that students must process the information themselves helps them develop flexible thinking and the habit of listening with understanding and empathy.

5. Causing students to analyze a task, decide on what is needed, and then act autonomously helps them with their social thinking and builds their questioning skills.

6. Causing others to define their terms, become specific about their actions, make precise comparisons, and use accurate descriptors represents the habit of thinking and communicating with clarity and precision.

7. Causing the covert thought processes that students are experiencing to become overt develops the habit of thinking about thinking (metacognition).

8. Employing positive presuppositions to enhance self-concept reinforces the dispositions necessary for habits of mind.

9. Helping children study and become alert to language cues that evoke thought processes develops their ability to gather data through all senses.

We stimulate and enhance others' thinking by asking questions, selecting terms, clarifying ideas and processes, providing data, and withholding value judgments. These strategies all contribute to mindful language, which is the language we use to grow intelligent behavior.

REFERENCES

Astington, S., & Olson, D. (1990). Metacognition and metalinguistic language: Learning to talk about thought. *Applied Psychology: An International Review (39)*1, 77–87.

Bailis, M., & Hunter, M. (1985, August 14). Do your words get them to think? *Learning*.

Beyer, B. (1991). Practical strategies for the direct teaching of thinking skills. In A. Costa (Ed.), *Developing minds: A resource book for teaching thinking* (Rev. ed., Vol.

1, pp. 274–279). Alexandria, VA: Association for Supervision and Curriculum Development.

Costa, A. (1984, November). Mediating the metacognitive. *Educational Leadership (42)*3, 57–62.

Costa, A., & Marzano, R. (1991). Teaching the language of thinking. In A. Costa (Ed.), *Developing minds: A resource book for teaching thinking* (Rev. ed., Vol. 1, pp. 251–254). Alexandria, VA: Association for Supervision and Curriculum Development.

Elgin, S. (1980). *The gentle art of verbal self-defense.* New York: Dorset Press.

Feuerstein, R. (1980). *Instrumental enrichment.* Baltimore, MD: University Park Press.

Flavell, J. (1977). *Cognitive development.* Edgewood Cliffs, NJ: Prentice-Hall.

Lipton, L., & Wellman, B. (1999). *Pathways to understanding.* Guilford, VT: Pathways Publishing.

Marzano, R., & Hutchins, C. L. (1985). *Thinking skills: A conceptual framework.* Aurora, CO: Mid-continent Research for Education and Learning.

Sternberg, R., & Caruso, D. (1985). Practical modes of knowing. In E. Eisner (Ed.), *Learning and teaching the ways of knowing* (pp. 133–158). 84th yearbook of the National Society for the Study of Education. Chicago, IL: University of Chicago Press.

Vygotsky, L. S. (1962). *Thought and language.* Cambridge, MA: Massachusetts Institute of Technology Press.

Whimbey, A. (1985). Test results from teaching thinking. In A. Costa (Ed.), *Developing minds: A resource book for teaching thinking* (pp. 269–271). Alexandria, VA: Association for Supervision and Curriculum Development.

3

USING QUESTIONS TO CHALLENGE STUDENTS' INTELLECT

ARTHUR L. COSTA AND BENA KALLICK

Thinking is an engagement of the mind that changes the mind.
Martin Heiddeger, *What Do We Mean*

When we ask teachers what they want their students to be able to do, they invariably emphasize the importance of thinking and problem solving. Yet given the high degree of apathy among today's students, how can we engage students' minds or, as Sizer (1992, p. 73) suggests, guide them to "use their minds well"?

A student's mind generally is engaged through some form of cognitive dissonance: a provocation or an inquiry. Effective teachers create this dissonance in two ways: (1) by raising a point of uncertainty or discrepancy in the content or (2) by pressing students to raise such points as they try to understand what is being presented. Ultimately, engagement occurs through student interest, and we can only foster the conditions in which students' interest might be piqued.

Questioning strategies provide a rich opportunity for developing student engagement. All questioning should focus on drawing students into the learning process. Learners must be presented with problems and questions, the answers to which are not readily known, if they are to become aware of, draw forth, practice, and apply the habits of mind.

Careful, intentional, productive questioning is one of the most powerful tools a skillful teacher possesses. Engaging students by posing questions is a clear signal that you are "democratizing" knowledge in the room, which conveys that every student is capable of knowing. When a teacher begins a question with, "Who can tell me . . . ?" it immediately signals that only certain students have the answer. If the teacher begins the question with, "What do we know about . . . ?" the words signal that all students have something to offer. If a teacher poses questions to which the answers already are known, students try to guess what's in the teacher's head and search for conformity or agreement. But if neither the teacher nor the students know the answers, they can share sincere, collaborative inquiry as they search for solutions.

This chapter describes powerful questioning strategies. We would like to equip teachers with the linguistic skills and metacognitive maps

- To monitor their own questions.
- To formulate and pose questions that intentionally challenge students' intellect and imagination.
- To encourage students' use of one or more of the habits of mind.

Remember that one of the ultimate purposes of posing questions is to help students increase their own habit of questioning and posing problems. To encourage such development, teachers must intentionally model complex questions in their own language.

SOME QUESTIONING "DON'TS"

We start by inviting teachers to heighten their awareness of their current questioning patterns. Are you miscuing, confusing, or limiting student thought? Some questions limit other people's thinking. These limits must be avoided for students (and adults) to use the habits of mind.

At least five types of questions miscue students' thinking because the questions send confusing and mixed messages. They do not belong in lessons designed to engage the habits of mind. Here are examples:

1. *Verification questions*, the answers to which already are known by you or by the student:
    - "What is the name of . . . ?"
    - "How many times did you . . . ?"

2. *Closed questions*, which can be answered "yes," "no," or "I can":
    - "Can you recite the poem?"
    - "Can you tell us the name of . . . ?"

- "Who can remember . . . ?"
- "Who can state the formula for . . . ?"

3. *Rhetorical questions* in which the answer is given within the question:
   - "In what year was the War of 1812?"
   - "Since when has Mikhail Gorbachev had his birthmark?"
   - "Who led Sherman's march through Georgia?"
   - "How long did the Seven Years War last?"

4. *Defensive questions*, which lead to justification, resistance, and self-protection:
   - "Why didn't you complete your homework?"
   - "Why would you do a thing like that?"
   - "Are you misbehaving again?"

5. *Agreement questions*, the intent of which is to invite others to agree with an opinion or answer:
   - "This is really the best solution, isn't it?"
   - "Let's do it my way, okay?"
   - "We really should get started now, shouldn't we?"
   - "Who can name the three basic parts of a plant? Root, stems, and leaves, right?"

QUESTIONS THAT CHALLENGE COMPLEX THINKING

Questions invite different levels and complexity of thinking. Early in children's lives, they learn to be alert to certain syntax cues to know how to behave or think. Teachers will want to use linguistic tools deliberately to engage and challenge complex thinking. The following vignette by Oliver Wendell Holmes captures the levels of thinking at increasingly complex levels (Costa, 1991, p. 178):

The Three-Story Intellect

There are one-story intellects, two-story intellects, and three-story intellects with skylights.

All fact collectors, who have no aim beyond their facts, are one-story men.

Two-story men compare, reason, generalize, using the labors of the fact collectors as well as their own.

36

Three-story men idealize, imagine, predict—their best illumination comes from above, through the skylight.

Holmes reminds us that all three levels of thinking are important. Teachers will want to design and pose questions that elicit all three levels of intellect. The graphic representation of Holmes's story in Figure 3.1 (see p. 38) can be used as a mental map to help teachers pose questions.

On the first story are the data-gathering cognitive operations. On the second story, we find cognitive operations that help students make meaning of the data: the processing level. The third story of the house invites students to go beyond the skylights to speculate, elaborate, and apply concepts in new and hypothetical situations. We offer examples of questions that invite specific cognitive operations at each level of the three-story intellect.

Data Gathering

Data-gathering questions are designed to draw from students the concepts, information, feelings, or experiences acquired in the past and stored in long- or short-term memory. These questions can also be designed to activate the senses to gather data for processing at the next higher level. Several cognitive processes are included at this level of thinking: recalling, completing, identifying, observing, counting, listing, reciting, defining, matching, scanning, describing, naming, and selecting. Examples of questions and statements designed to elicit these cognitive objectives are

- "Name the states that border California." [Naming]
- "How does the picture make you feel?" [Describing]
- "What word does this picture go with?" [Matching]
- "Define the word *haggard*." [Defining]
- "What did you see the man doing in the film?" [Observing]
- "Which ball is the blue one?" [Identifying]
- "How does the Gettysburg Address begin?" [Reciting]
- "How many coins are in the stack?" [Counting]
- "Which words in this list rhyme?" [Selecting]
- "The Mexican houses were made of mud bricks called . . . what?" [Completing]
- "Watch what color it turns when I put the litmus paper in the liquid." [Observing]
- "List the first four numbers in a set of positive integers." [Listing]
- "How did you feel about the grade you received in science?" [Recalling]

FIGURE 3.1
The Three-Story Intellect Model

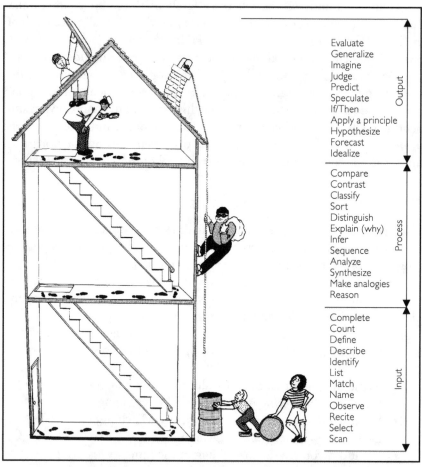

Evaluate
Generalize
Imagine
Judge
Predict
Speculate
If/Then
Apply a principle
Hypothesize
Forecast
Idealize

Output

Compare
Contrast
Classify
Sort
Distinguish
Explain (why)
Infer
Sequence
Analyze
Synthesize
Make analogies
Reason

Process

Complete
Count
Define
Describe
Identify
List
Match
Name
Observe
Recite
Select
Scan

Input

Adapted by permission of the publisher from the "Three-Story Intellect Model" from *Brain Compatible Classrooms* by Robin Fogarty, © 1997 SkyLight Training and Publishing, Inc.

PROCESSING

Teachers can guide students to process data in many ways. Sometimes teachers design questions and statements to seek cause-and-effect relationships. Other questions lead students to synthesize, analyze, summarize, compare, contrast, or classify. Several other cognitive processes are included at this level of thinking: distinguishing, making analogies, categorizing, experimenting, organizing, explaining, sequencing, grouping, and inferring. Examples of questions designed to elicit cognitive objectives at the processing level are

- "In what ways do you see the Civil War like the Revolutionary War?" [Comparing]
- "What suggests to you that Columbus believed he could get to the East by sailing west?" [Explaining]
- "From our experiments with food coloring in different water temperatures, what might you infer about the movement of molecules?" [Inferring]
- "How might you arrange the rocks in the order of their size?" [Sequencing]
- "What do you think caused the liquid to turn blue?" [Explaining]
- "Arrange in groups the things that a magnet will and will not pick up." [Grouping]
- "What other machines can you think of that work in the same way that this one does?" [Making analogies]
- "What are some characteristics of Van Gogh's work that make you think this painting is his?" [Distinguishing]
- "What might you do to test your idea?" [Experimenting]
- "In what ways are pine needles different from redwood needles?" [Contrasting]
- "In what ways might you arrange the blocks so that they have a crowded effect?" [Organizing]
- "What data are we going to need to solve this problem?" [Analyzing]
- "Arrange the following elements of a set in ascending order: 13/4, 3/2, 5/6, 32/5." [Sequencing]
- "How does the formula for finding the volume of a cone compare with the formula for the volume of a pyramid?" [Comparing]

This level of cognition also is important when students conduct research projects. Often, students simply copy or paraphrase the text in a resource book. When students understand that research is, by definition, inquiry, they learn to raise questions that can be answered only through true research. The cognitive processes listed at the start of this section can guide students to raise questions at a more complex level. Thus, an assignment might read, "As you *analyze* the development of machines, what were some of their *effects* on the people living at that time?" Or, "In what way does the main character in this novel *compare* to the main character in that novel?"

If you're planning a whole unit, an essential question at this level might read: "How did the invention of the wheel affect our lives today?"

SPECULATING, ELABORATING, AND APPLYING CONCEPTS

Other questions and statements are designed to have students go beyond the concept or principle and use it in a novel or hypothetical situation. This application invites students to think creatively and hypothetically, to use their imagination, to expose a value system, or to make a judgment. These questions lend themselves most powerfully to the research process because their answers cannot be found in books or other data sources. Students must make sense of the resource material and answer an inquiry that requires them to invest in the material. Verbs that describe this cognitive level include applying, imagining, evaluating, judging, hypothesizing, generalizing, model building, predicting, extrapolating, speculating, forecasting, and transferring. For example, consider these questions:

• "What do you suppose will happen to our weather if a high pressure area moves in?" [Forecasting]
• "If our population continues to grow as it does, what do you suppose life will be like in the 22nd century?" [Speculating]
• "Because the amount of heat does affect the speed of movement of the molecules, what do you think will happen when we put the liquid in the refrigerator?" [Predicting]
• "Imagine what life would be like if we had no laws to govern us." [Imagining]
• "What might you say about all countries' economies that are dependent upon only one crop?" [Generalizing]
• "Design a way to use this bimetal strip to make a fire alarm." [Applying]
• "How could you use this clay to make a model of a plant cell?" [Model building]
• "What would be a fair solution to this problem?" [Evaluating]
• "What makes this painting unique?" [Judging]
• "Given what we have learned, what other examples of romantic music can you cite?" [Applying]
• "What do you think might happen if we placed the saltwater fish in the tank of fresh water?" [Hypothesizing]

Here are typical research questions at this level:

• "As you consider the periodic table and the invention of the microscope, which was more essential to organizing chemistry?"
• "How is the current trend in rap music another form of poetry?"
• "How were the inventions of the industrial age a necessary form of development for a culture?"

An essential question at this level might sound like this: "Is there such a thing as a 'good' war?"

COMPOSING POWERFUL QUESTIONS

Desirable questions elicit in students an awareness and engagement of the habits of mind. These kinds of questions have three characteristics (Costa & Garmston, 1999):

1. *The questions are invitational.* The teacher uses an approachable voice. There is a lilt and melody in the questioner's voice rather than a flat, even tenor. Plurals are used to invite multiple, rather than singular, concepts:
   - "What are *some* of your *goals*?"
   - "What *ideas* do you have?"
   - "What *outcomes* do you seek?"
   - "What *alternatives* are you considering?"

The teacher selects words to express tentativeness:
   - "What conclusions *might* you draw?"
   - "What *may* indicate his acceptance?"
   - "What *hunches* do you have to explain this situation?"

The teacher also uses invitational stems to enable the behavior to be performed:
   - "As you *think* about . . . ."
   - "As you *consider* . . . ."
   - "As you *reflect* on . . . ."

Positive presuppositions assume capability and empowerment:
   - "What are *some* of the *benefits you will derive* from *engaging* in this activity?"
   - "*As you anticipate* your project, what will be *some indicators* that you are progressing and *succeeding*?"

2. *The questions engage specific cognitive operations, as described in the three levels: data gathering; processing; and speculating, elaborating, and applying concepts.*

3. *The questions address content that is either external or internal to the person being addressed.* External content might be what is going on in the

environment around the student: lesson content, another student, a project, or a playground or home experience. Internal content might be what is going on inside the student's mind: satisfaction, puzzlement, frustration, thinking processes (metacognition), feelings, or emotions.

Let's put these three elements together. Teachers can compose powerful questions using an invitational stem, a cognitive operation, and content.

First, choose an invitational stem:

- As you . . . .
- What are some of . . . .
- How might you . . . .
- What led to . . . .
- What possible . . . .
- What might . . . .
- How might . . . .
- How should . . . .

Next, name the cognitive operation. At the data-gathering level, choose words such as

- Recall
- Define
- Describe
- Identify
- Name
- List

At the processing level, use words such as

- Compare/Contrast
- Infer
- Analyze
- Sequence
- Synthesize
- Summarize

At the level where students should speculate, elaborate, and apply concepts, use words such as

- Predict
- Evaluate

- Speculate
- Imagine
- Envision
- Hypothesize

In seeking internal content, ask about

- Reaction
- Feelings
- Thoughts
- Emotions

In seeking external content, ask about

- Project
- Other students
- Group
- Event
- Goals
- Lesson

Consider these rich, complex questions:

- "As you compare this project with others that you have done . . . ."
- "How might you sequence these events in such a way as to . . . ?"
- "What led you to these inferences about your performance's success?"
- "In what ways might your emotions have influenced your decisions about . . . ?"

ENGAGING THE HABITS OF MIND

If we want students to become aware of and to practice the habits of mind, teachers and parents must learn to pose questions that help children draw forth or become aware of one or more of the habits. We offer examples of "categorical questions" that are intended to invite someone else to draw forth one of the habits of mind. Please notice the invitational stems, positive presuppositions, plural and tentative language, level of cognition, and content. Here are examples, with the specific habit of mind shown in brackets:

- "While you were reading, what was going on inside your head to monitor your comprehension of the story?" [Thinking about thinking (metacognition)]
- "If you were John, how do you think he would react to what you said about him?" [Listening with understanding and empathy]
- "What are some other ways you could solve this problem?" [Thinking flexibly]
- "What questions will you ask to gather the data you need to solve this problem?" [Questioning and posing problems]
- "How do you know your answer is correct?" [Striving for accuracy]
- "What intrigues you about this experiment?" [Responding with wonderment and awe]

The following cross-categorical questions are intended to invite someone to draw upon at least two or more of the habits of mind:

- "As you listen to others' points of view, what metacognitive strategies do you employ to see the situation from their perspective?" [Thinking about thinking (metacognition); listening with understanding and empathy; thinking flexibly]
- "As you read, what do you do when your mind wanders but you want to remain on task?" [Persisting; thinking about thinking (metacognition)]
- "When you find yourself tempted to respond emotionally to a situation, what alternatives do you consider?" [Managing impulsivity; thinking flexibly]
- "When you are communicating with others, what indicators are you aware of in yourself and others that signal you are being understood?" [Thinking and communicating with clarity and precision; thinking about thinking (metacognition)]
- "As you talk to yourself about this problem, what new insights were generated?" [Thinking about thinking (metacognition); creating, imagining, innovating]

Skillful teachers compose and monitor their questions with the specific intention of having students engage one or more of the habits of mind. These kinds of questions build heightened consciousness. Students hear the specific vocabulary, and they soon learn that the habits are valued and can be used throughout their lives.

REFERENCES

Costa, A. (1991). *The school as a home for the mind.* Palatine, IL: SkyLight Publishers.

Costa, A., & Garmston, R. (1999). *Cognitive coaching: A foundation for Renaissance schools.* Norwood, MA: Christopher Gordon Publishers.

Sizer, T. R. (1992). *Horace's school.* New York: Houghton Mifflin Co.

4

THINKING MAPS: VISUAL TOOLS FOR ACTIVATING HABITS OF MIND

DAVID HYERLE

New theories penetrate into the world of practical affairs when they are translated into methods and tools. . . . "Tool" comes from a prehistoric Germanic word for "to make, to prepare, or to do." It still carries that meaning: Tools are what you make, prepare, or do with.

Peter Senge

In early 1995, 4th graders at Friendship Valley Elementary School in Carroll County, Maryland, responded to a narrative writing prompt on the Maryland Performance-Based Assessment. The school had been built five years before on the principles of the "School as a Home for the Mind" (Costa, 1991), and it had strengthened its program through a range of high-quality teaching and learning strategies.

If you had been standing in a certain hallway of Friendship Valley on the morning of that test—normally a stressful few hours for all involved—you would have been startled by an ecstatic teacher running out of a room exclaiming, "They're using them on the test!" Many of her students, without coaching, had used Thinking Maps® to generate and organize information to complete the prompt. After the testing documents were collected, the teacher asked students to write about strategies they used during the test. One student responded with a note and a flow map, one of the eight Thinking Maps that students had been taught (see Figure 4.1).

By the time the student and her peers sat down for the writing test, they were relatively fluent with using the flow map to direct and construct networks of knowledge on the way to final products. In addition, they had developed the disposition for creativity and flexibility. They were able to persist, and they could call on a highly developed system for reflection and metacognition. In the end, these students' test scores were second across the whole state of Maryland on the combined scoring of six performance assessments—well beyond the mark where students in the school had performed previously. Exactly how was it that the student and her classmates, in the midst of a stressful test, were able to pull up a Thinking Map in their mind's eye?

FIGURE 4.1

Student Flow Map

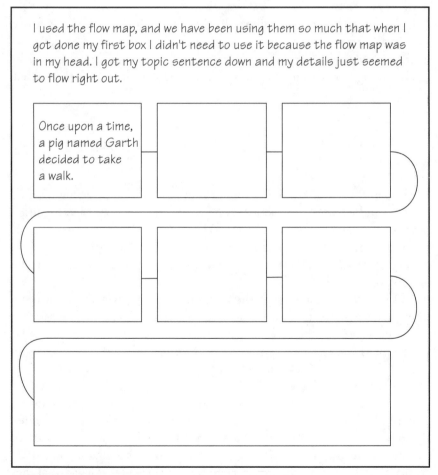

Source: Adapted from Hyerle, 2000a.

THE VISUAL BRAIN

The brain is capable of absorbing 36,000 images every minute. How can this incredible figure be true? It is because the sophisticated, front-loaded wiring of our brain system is well beyond our imagination. Research approximates that between 80 and 90 percent of the information received by the brain is through the eyes. Though our auditory and kinesthetic modes of sensing are complex and integrated with visual processing, the dominant mode is visual. Such dominance may seem a radical departure from the idea that we need to somehow balance instruction across multiple modalities. Yet the reality is that the human brain has evolved to become positively *imbalanced* toward visual imaging for information processing.

Even if we believe that some individuals are more kinesthetic, auditory, or visual learners—or more global or analytic—we need to consider research showing that each of us still processes far more information visually than through other modalities. We must help students use their visual strengths.

VISUAL TOOLS FOR CONSTRUCTING KNOWLEDGE

Metacognition means thinking about thinking. It means knowing what we know—and what we don't know—and how we know that. Metacognition also refers to an awareness and control of one's cognitive processes and the regulatory mechanisms used to problem solve. Metacognition anchors strategies for students so that they can apply them in life situations beyond school.

When students represent their cognitive strategies with visual tools, they practice metacognition, a principle of learning where they describe the thinking processes they use to pattern content knowledge and to solve problems (Hyerle, 1996). Three types of visual tools aid this metacognition: brainstorming webs, task-specific graphic organizers, and thinking-process maps (see Figure 4.2).

Carpenters and chefs have particular tools for different operations; so, too, thinkers turn to different visual tools to activate certain habits of mind. In the examples that follow, we see that students can develop their capacities to be creative and flexible, to persevere, to be systematic, and to be aware of and reflective about metacognitive patterns to the degree that they can fluently apply these patterns to classroom challenges.

FIGURE 4.2

Constructing Knowledge

Types of Visual Tools		
Brainstorming Webs	**Task-Specific Graphic Organizers**	**Thinking-Process Maps**
Webbing	Story boards	Concept mapping
Mindmapping	Time lines	Systems diagrams
Clustering	Problem-Solution	Thinking Maps

Source: Adapted from Hyerle, 2000a.

The graphic representations in Figure 4.3 (see p. 50), or "displayed metacognition" (Costa, 1991), enable students to look into their own thinking as they might look at their own reflection in a pool of water. With visual tools, students see their thinking displayed. From this public display, all students can readily share in one another's thinking and become self-reflective on the process, content, and, most importantly, evolving *form* of their thinking.

BRAINSTORMING WEBS

Although brainstorming webs appear in infinite forms, most learners start in the center of a blank page and branch out, creating idiosyncratic designs as an idea expands. The open form and purpose of brainstorming webs promote creative generation of ideas without blinders. Most brainstorming webs are used for thinking "outside the box," and they spark a high degree of open-ended networking and associative thinking.

After students become fluent with webbing, or with Tony Buzan's more specific techniques called Mindmapping™ (Buzan, 1994), it becomes clear that a cluster of intelligent behaviors, centered around creative thinking, is actively engaged and facilitated. Although educators have found it easy to identify verbal and written fluency as key objectives in school, it is more

FIGURE 4.3
Visual Tools and the Habits of Mind

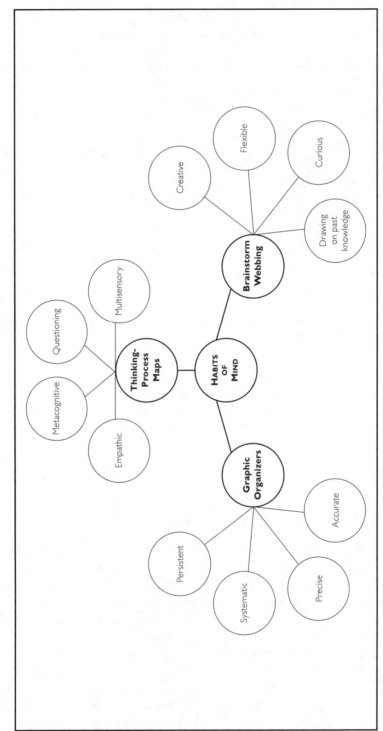

Source: Adapted from Hyerle, 1999.

difficult for us to see that these two forms—speech and writing—are essentially linear representations. With brainstorming webs, students have self-generated, nonlinear tools for activating fluent thinking, which reflects the holistic networking capacity of the human brain.

Students call upon their disposition for ingenuity, originality, and insightfulness to express this form of thinking. Brainstorming webs provide the tools for venturing to the edge of our thinking—and thinking beyond the edge. Brainstorming also opens other habits of mind such as flexibility and curiosity.

Many teachers have a particular concern about brainstorming: What happens after the storm? Students need to move beyond the generation of ideas. They need to gain organizational control over ideas, and they need self-control to support more systematic and analytical thinking. To address this concern, another type of visual tool supports another cluster of habits of mind.

TASK-SPECIFIC GRAPHIC ORGANIZERS

Unlike webs, which facilitate thinking *outside* the box, most graphic organizers are structured so that students think *inside* the box. A teacher may create or take from a teacher's guide a specific visual structure that students follow and fill in as they proceed through a complex series of steps. Teachers often match these organizers with specific patterns of content or the development of content skills; thus, they are called task-specific organizers. These highly structured graphics may seem constraining at times, yet each can be fruitful for students as they systematically approach a task, organize their ideas, and stay focused (especially when the task is complex).

For example, many organizers are sequential, showing the steps for solving a word problem, organizing content information for a research report, learning a specific process for a certain kind of writing prompt, or highlighting essential skills and patterns for comprehending a story. Because these types of visual tools are highly structured, they directly facilitate several habits of mind: persisting, managing impulsivity, striving for accuracy, and thinking and communicating with clarity and precision.

The visual/spatial structure guides students through the steps, box by box or oval by oval. Teachers report that one of the main outcomes of using graphic organizers is that they provide a concrete system and model for proceeding through a problem that students would otherwise abandon because they have not developed their own organizational structures for persisting. An obvious reason for this advantage is that the visual structure reveals a whole view of the process and, importantly, an end point.

This kind of structuring also provides visual guidelines, much like a rope students can grasp. They don't impulsively jump outside the problem to what Benjamin Bloom calls "one-shot thinking." The visual modeling shows students that they can manage their impulsivity and stay in the box when they need to focus on following through to a solution. This kind of modeling also lends itself to greater accuracy and precision of language. Students usually don't have a record of their thinking, along with the steps and missteps they took along the way. They also have a hard time differentiating one idea from the next. By visually capturing their thinking, students can look back on their ideas, refine them, and share them with others to get feedback.

Both brainstorming webs and graphic organizers help students become familiar and fluent with networking and patterning information. Such work leads to a question about the relationships between thinking skills instruction and visual tools: Are there common patterns of thinking keyed to questions we ask every day in schools that could—if represented visually—deepen students' understanding and extension of their own thinking and habits of mind?

THINKING-PROCESS MAPS

A third kind of visual tool now appearing in classrooms simultaneously supports thinking inside and outside the box. These tools—which I call thinking-process maps—are designed to reflect common patterns of thinking, from fundamental cognitive skills such as comparison, classification, and cause-effect reasoning to integrated visual languages such as Concept Mapping™ (Novak & Gowin, 1984), systems diagramming, and Thinking Maps.

Although these dynamic tools often *look* much like some static graphic organizers we see in classrooms, the differences in the purpose, introduction, application, and outcomes are significant. Thinking-process maps scaffold many habits of mind related to brainstorming webs and organizers, but these tools focus explicitly on different forms of concept development. They facilitate more explicitly four habits of mind: questioning and posing problems, gathering data through all senses, thinking about thinking (metacognition), and listening with understanding and empathy.

As one example, let's look at Thinking Maps, a synthesis model, or *language*, of eight thinking-process maps. This toolbox of visual tools combines the creative thinking facilitated by brainstorming webs, the organizational structures of graphic organizers, and the metacognitive capacities inherent in thinking-process maps, such as concept mapping and systems diagramming. As shown in the descriptions provided in Figure 4.4, each map is grounded in a specific, fundamental cognitive process. When used as connected tools—on a blank piece of paper, a chalkboard, a white board, or with Thinking Maps software (*Thinking Maps: Technology for Learning*, 1998)—these maps concretely support interactive teaching, higher-order thinking and learning, and assessing across linear and nonlinear patterns of knowledge.

FIGURE 4.4

Thinking Maps: A Common Visual Language

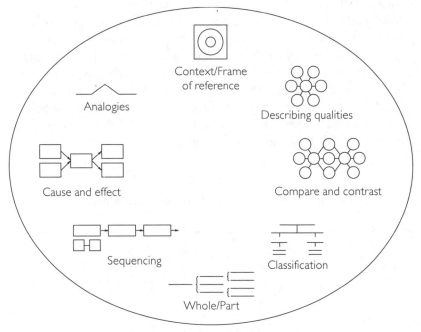

Reprinted by permission of the publisher from *Thinking Maps® Training of Trainers Resource Manual* by David Hyerle, © 2000 Innovative Sciences, Inc.

For a concrete example of Thinking Maps at work, consider this learning objective a teacher in New York City gave to her 5th grade class: "In celebration of Black History Month, research and write a report on a famous African American." This teacher knew that the cognitive complexity of this multistep process was daunting to her students. But all teachers and students in this inner-city, K–5 school had been trained for years in the use of Thinking Maps, and they had applied these tools across disciplines. By the time the 5th grade students faced this objective, they were fluent with all eight tools for patterning thinking in reading, writing, and mathematics. They also had learned how to use multiple maps together to create final products. Figures 4.5, 4.6, and 4.7 (see p. 56) show how one student independently used Thinking Maps as tools for writing an essay for her investigation of the life of Frederick Douglass.

First, the student used a bubble map to identify key attributes about Frederick Douglass (Figure 4.5). This map is based on the cognitive skill of identifying attributes of things and developing a descriptive cluster of qualities of the man: dedicated, smart, courageous, and determined. The student then used the tree map to sort the information into the paper topic, the supporting ideas, and a detailed factual record (Figure 4.6). The tree map helped her synthesize a vast quantity of ideas while deleting extraneous details. Last, she used a flow map to create a logical progression of ideas for writing (Figure 4.7). The outcome from these Thinking Maps was a highly scored 10-paragraph essay that mirrored the flow map. Additionally, the three maps also were submitted in typed form providing evidence of the thinking processes she went through on the way to the final product.

Consider now the three types of visual tools and the clusters of behaviors related to each. First, this student investigated Frederick Douglass, starting with blank pages and developing map after map of ideas drawn

FIGURE 4.5
Using a Bubble Map to Identify Attributes

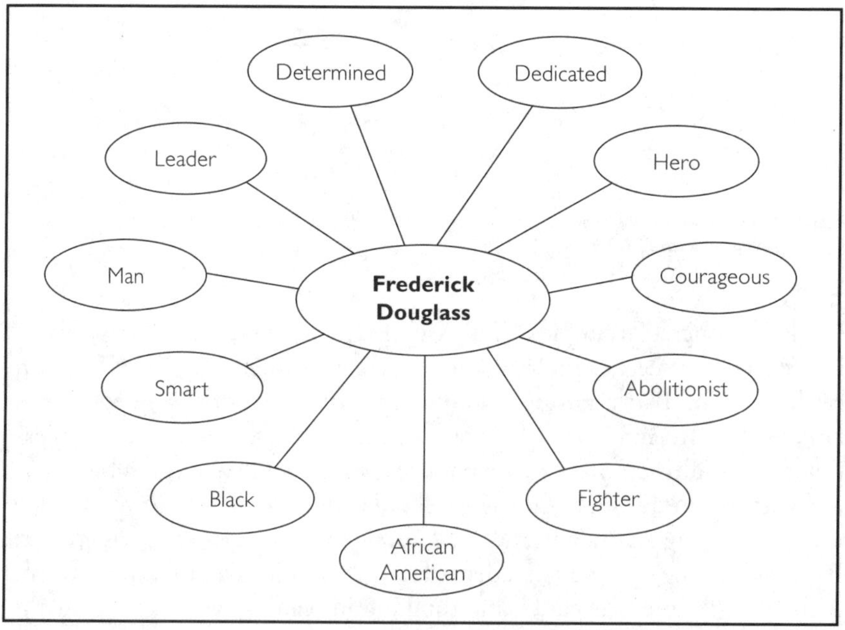

Source: Hyerle, 2000a.

from resources in the school. She linked information from map to map as well, easily transforming information into different patterns of thought. Even though the bubble map is specifically intended for identifying attributes or characteristics, it provided a way for the student to abstract Douglass's essential qualities from linear textual sources and develop a rich cluster of information.

Second, much as with graphic organizers, this student shows that the starting points—or common graphic primitives—for each Thinking Map effectively facilitate perseverance in the task. The student stayed focused on the lengthy, multistep requirements of the project: research, organization, and writing.

FIGURE 4.6
Using a Tree Map to Sort Information

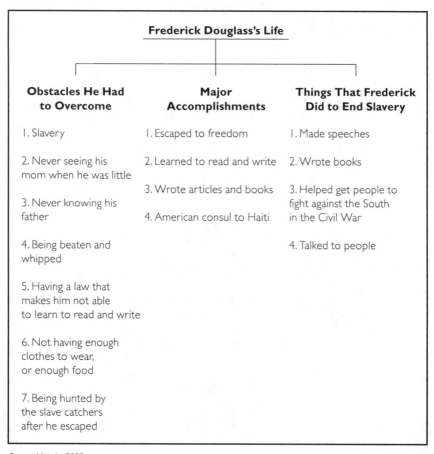

Frederick Douglass's Life

Obstacles He Had to Overcome	Major Accomplishments	Things That Frederick Did to End Slavery
1. Slavery	1. Escaped to freedom	1. Made speeches
2. Never seeing his mom when he was little	2. Learned to read and write	2. Wrote books
3. Never knowing his father	3. Wrote articles and books	3. Helped get people to fight against the South in the Civil War
4. Being beaten and whipped	4. American consul to Haiti	4. Talked to people
5. Having a law that makes him not able to learn to read and write		
6. Not having enough clothes to wear, or enough food		
7. Being hunted by the slave catchers after he escaped		

Source: Hyerle, 2000a.

Third, as with other thinking-process maps, this student became aware of the multiple cognitive processes necessary for completing the task. She developed fluency with the tools that enabled her to configure the Thinking Maps to match her evolving understandings about Frederick Douglass. She "chunked" information and consciously formed the information into different patterns, which enabled her to write the essay. This process is atypical of what most students can do, especially when they are confronted with the otherwise daunting learning objective of researching, organizing, and then writing an essay report.

FIGURE 4.7

Using a Flow Map to Pull It All Together

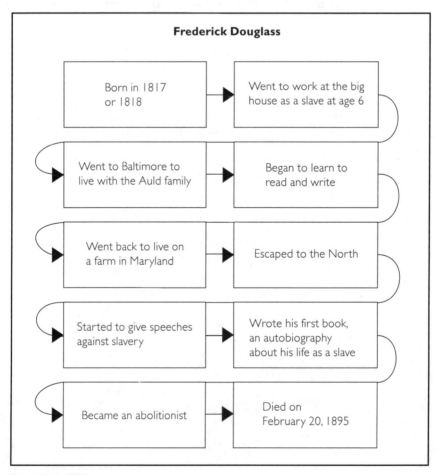

Source: Hyerle, 2000a.

EFFECTS OF USING THINKING MAPS

Teachers, students, and administrators report some or all of these outcomes after implementing Thinking Maps:

- Increased memory of content knowledge when reading.
- Well-organized final products, particularly written work.
- Deeper conceptual understandings.
- Greater capacity to communicate abstract concepts.
- Heightened metacognition and self-assessment.
- Enhanced creativity and perspective.
- Transfer of thinking processes across disciplines and outside school.
- Test-score changes in reading, writing, and mathematics (Hyerle, 2000a).

Such learning was brought home to a teacher in North Carolina when her 10th grade students started using multiple Thinking Maps to interpret and then write a formal character analysis for a Langston Hughes short story, "Thank You, Ma'm." One student, who had struggled with writing all year, told the teacher, "The maps have helped me see what you mean when you tell us to go beyond the surface of the story and think deeply. I didn't think I could, but when I created the map I realized that I could have those kinds of ideas. The writing is much easier now." This student's experience summarizes one of the most important educational goals of all: When students combine the use of visual tools with the habits of mind to think more deeply, they *see* their own expanding ideas and thus gain a new sense of themselves as efficacious thinkers.

REFERENCES

Buzan, T. (1994). *Use both sides of your brain.* London: Dutton.

Costa, A. (1991). Foreword. In J. Clark, *Patterns of thinking.* New York: Allyn and Bacon.

Hyerle, D. (1996). *Visual tools for constructing knowledge.* Alexandria, VA: Association for Supervision and Curriculum Development.

Hyerle, D. (1999). *Visual tools and technologies* [Videotape]. Lyme, NH: Designs for Thinking.

Hyerle, D. (2000a). *A field guide to using visual tools.* Alexandria, VA: Association for Supervision and Curriculum Development.

Hyerle, D. (2000b). *Thinking Maps® training of trainers resource manual*. Raleigh, NC: Innovative Sciences.

Novak, J., & Gowin, R. (1984). *Learning how to learn*. Cambridge, MA: Cambridge University Press.

Thinking Maps®: Technology for learning [Software]. (1998). Raleigh, NC: Innovative Sciences.

5

INFUSING HABITS OF MIND INTO UNITS, LESSONS, AND LEARNING TASKS

ARTHUR L. COSTA AND BENA KALLICK

Teachers have an opportunity to make habits of mind a significant part of classroom work whenever they develop units of study, design lessons, or create learning tasks. Our experiences in the field have shown that habits of mind make the most sense when they are integrated as a part of the entire working process in a classroom.

Experience has shown, too, that clusters of habits go together naturally. Teachers will not—and should not—teach all 16 habits at once. Instead, they can select which habits to incorporate based upon their assessment of students' needs, the content and context of the lesson, and other school priorities. Think of the habits of mind as a smorgasbord: You have a vast array from which to choose. Which of the habits pique your interest, and which of the habits are likely to satisfy your students' hunger to learn?

This chapter contains examples of how thoughtful classroom practitioners have designed units, lessons, and learning tasks that incorporate both content and one or more of the habits of mind. You will notice design differences between a lesson, which can be accomplished in a short time, and a unit, which can be extended over a long period. A series of lessons and activities often serve as scaffolding for a larger theme or unit of study. When choosing such themes, it is important to work with content that lends itself to generating many questions, ideas, and interpretations. We have found that the most generative topics or themes have these characteristics:

• They interest the student.
• They offer a pathway for students to find a relationship between their own experience and the content to be studied.

- They present problems that have not yet been solved.
- They have more than one interpretation or point of view.
- They are universal, not particular, in meaning.
- They require both primary and secondary source material.
- They interest both teacher and students.
- They have not been studied previously from the same perspective.

As this list demonstrates, themes or topics that fulfill these characteristics are worthy of more time and attention than most individual lessons might be. They help students think in larger ways about the material they are studying, and they provide a rich opportunity for students to practice the habits of mind.

Unit Design

Many teachers find the framework in Figure 5.1 helpful as they plan units. This framework focuses on critical planning elements, and that planning usually begins with brainstorming. Which topic or theme are you most interested in expanding into a unit? To which aspect of the curriculum can you devote more time and depth for study? Once you have decided what you want students to know, be able to do, and become intrigued with as a result of this unit, project, or problem, fill in your own organizational form, using the one in Figure 5.1 as a model. Figure 5.2 (see p. 63) shows how a team of 6th grade social studies teachers from New Paltz Middle School, New Paltz, New York, used this form for a geography unit.

The following examples were collected from teachers in schools that use the unit design illustrated in Figures 5.1 and 5.2. For the first example, we have provided guided commentary in italics. For the other examples, you may want to create your own commentary to help you better understand how the teachers have integrated habits of mind and content.

Example 1: Lake Wilderness Elementary School

Following a design strategy helps teachers build units of study. First, they consider the unit outcome: "What is it that you want a student to know and be able to do as a result of this particular unit?" Next is to create a series of guiding questions. Each guiding question follows a pattern. The first part is the question; the second part is the specific skill or habit on which the teacher will focus.

FIGURE 5.1
Framework for a Unit Design

Theme/Topic			
Essential Questions			
Content	Processes and Skills	Habits of Mind	Assessment
What concepts, subjects, topics, or disciplines do you want students to comprehend?	Individual: (i.e., self-management skills) Thinking skills: (i.e., experimentation, hypothesis formation, comparing) Group: (i.e., collaboration skills)	Which two or three habits are needed to accomplish this task?	How will students demonstrate their mastery? Describe learning activities in which students will perform processes, content, and habits of mind.
List the most significant topics or concepts on which students will focus.	List the specific skills you want the students to practice and learn.	List the specific habits of mind that best fit this topic.	List indicators of performance and describe how they will be monitored and recorded.

For example, a team of 1st grade teachers from Lake Wilderness Elementary School in the Tahoma School District in Maple Valley, Washington, designed this unit outcome and several guiding questions.

Unit Outcome

Students will explore the community and culture of Australia in order to practice the skills of effective communicators and collaborative workers in a culturally diverse world.
Commentary: This is a statement of what the teacher wants the students to know and be able to do as a result of the study of this unit.

Guiding Questions

1. What challenges has Australia faced over time?
   • Historically
   • Environmentally
   • Currently

Teach **main idea** thinking skill.
Commentary: Notice how the teacher has incorporated specific thinking skills into her unit. Students can learn the skill and practice it as it is infused with the content.

2. What are the relationships that exist among the peoples of Australia?
  • Aborigines
  • European immigrants

Teach **effective communicator** learner outcome.
Commentary: The teacher is including the district essential learnings, which define life skills necessary when students exit high school.

3. What is unique about Australia?
  • Culture
  • Plants/Animals
  • Arts

4. How can we reflect our understanding of Australia through an independent project?
  • **Multiple intelligences** project.

Commentary: The teacher is incorporating her knowledge of brain research, learning styles, and Gardner's work on multiple intelligences. She is thoughtfully integrating an assessment project that will give students multiple ways of demonstrating what they have learned.

  • Project **self-reflection**.

Commentary: This project incorporates metacognition as a way for students to anchor their learning in self-reflection.

  • Teach **originality** and **metacognition** habits of mind.

Commentary: Because the project will call for originality (using multiple intelligences to create a product) and metacognition (for self-reflection), she teaches those habits of mind directly.

  • Teach **self-directed learner** student outcomes.

Commentary: The framework suggested in Figure 5.1 describes a way to think of outcomes developmentally, beginning with the activities that you want a student to engage with and continuing to the lifelong learning outcomes. Although

FIGURE 5.2
Unit Plan

Theme/Topic:
Geography—Eastern Hemisphere: "Where in the World?" Mountains and Molehills

Essential Questions

1. How does geography affect the culture, government, economy, and history of Africa, Asia, and Europe?

2. What are the major land forms, bodies of water, natural resources, and climate of the Eastern Hemisphere?

3. How do these factors influence peoples' lives?

4. How do the continents compare to one another?

Content	Processes and Skills	Habits of Mind	Assessment
How is geography different in Europe, Asia, and Africa? • Land forms • Natural resources • Climate • Bodies of water • Location	Compare and contrast. Identify and label on maps. Read and interpret climate maps.	Persisting Listening with understanding and empathy Striving for accuracy Thinking and communicating with clarity and precision	Students will teach two other students key concepts by preparing a graphic organizer, filling in a map, and showing pictures or other objects that help to explain the geographic themes of the continent they have become expert in. To check the two students' understanding, they will be asked to answer three questions using the framework as the basis for answering.

Source: A team of 6th grade social studies teachers at New Paltz Middle School, New Paltz, New York.

you can begin in either direction, the main point is that you consider each out-come as a part of your design work. This particular teacher integrates a combi-nation of thinking skills, lifelong learning skills, and habits of mind into the content of her study of Australia. Without the careful planning shown above, it would be difficult to weave all of the aspects of curriculum, instruction, and assessment into such a rich tapestry of learning.

EXAMPLE 2: EAU CLAIRE AREA SCHOOL DISTRICT

In the extended excerpt below, members of the Critical Thinking Leadership Team from the Eau Claire Area School District in Eau Claire, Wisconsin, describe how they incorporated habits of mind in a unit called "Geo City:"

> We sought to make thinking a habit by intentionally linking the habits of mind to every content area. When engaged in a project, students worked with both the vocabulary and concepts of the content and with the intelligent behaviors as applied to that situation. This experience pro-vided an ongoing self-assessment opportunity. An example of this idea is our work with "Geo City." You will see the content of geometry and the concept of intelligent behavior integrated in the examples described below.

Content Objective: The learner will be able to demonstrate knowledge of geometric shapes by creating a Geo City.

Content Criteria

    1. The surface area of your city must not be greater than 616 square inches.

    2. Your city must include one of each of these figures: cube, cylin-der, pyramid, rectangular prism, cone, and sphere. One building must consist of a combination of at least two shapes.

    3. Streets must be 1½ inches wide. They must intersect at three dif-ferent angles: right, obtuse, and acute.

    4. Include a body of water with at least one line of symmetry.

    5. Include parallel, perpendicular, and intersecting lines.

    6. Include a tessellation you have created.

    7. Add extras, such as trees, parks, and road signs.

    8. Name all streets and buildings, the body of water, and the city.

    9. Draw on graph paper a map of your city that uses symbols (color and shapes) and coordinates (latitude and longitude). Include a key for the symbols.

10. Create, design, and make a brochure that tells your city's best feature.

11. The design must first be agreed upon by both partners, drawn on scratch paper, and then approved by the teacher before work begins.

Content Evaluation
1. Completeness of tasks
2. Development of plan
3. Accuracy and precision
4. Description of product
5. Inventiveness and originality
6. Perseverance

Lifelong Learner Objective: The learner will be able to reflect upon his/her progress as a persistent, accurate, and creative thinker.

Lifelong Learner Criteria
1. Displays persistence and perseverance.
2. Checks for accuracy and precision.
3. Aware of own thinking (metacognition).
4. Produces work that reflects creative thinking.

Lifelong Learner Evaluation: Use a graphic organizer to monitor and self-assess progress.

Performance Levels for Content and Lifelong Learner Assessment Rubric
4 *Distinguished.* The student completes all important components, demonstrates in-depth understanding, and offers insightful extension in significant details.
3 *Proficient.* The student completes the most important component and understands major concepts but overlooks less important ideas.
2 *Apprentice.* The student completes some of the important components but there are gaps in his/her understanding.
1 *Novice.* The student shows minimal understanding, but he/she lacks clear communication and generates inaccurate or irrelevant information.

Geometric City Video Presentation
Congratulations! You have completed the building portion of your city. Here are some guidelines for your Geometric City video presentation:

1. Write and share the history of your city.

2. Include information about population, government, and cultural events.

3. Point out the geometric shapes you have designed. Mention the names of businesses or special features of your city.

4. Discuss where the required angles and lines are located.

5. Be creative. Add any important details you and your partner decide need to be mentioned.

6. During the videotaping of your city project, take turns telling about your city. Plan who will report the above information.

7. Practice your presentation before you make your video.

LESSON DESIGN

In Lisa Davis's classroom in West Orchard Elementary School, Chappaqua, New York, she designs specific lessons that require using certain habits of mind. For example, during a lesson on persistence, she asks students to answer questions, do activities, and complete a statement:

- What do you see a persistent person doing?
- What do you hear a persistent person saying?
- List the attributes (characteristics) of a person who is persistent.
- When would these attributes be helpful for you to practice?
- Persistence is like _____ because _____.
- Draw a picture to help others understand persistence.
- Write a catchy phrase or slogan to remind yourself and others to practice persistence.

At this point, she gives students a direct application of the habit in a well-planned lesson that incorporates both the content and the habit she wants students to use. In the following excerpt, the content is division of fractions, and the habit is persistence:

Math Persistence
Objective: Students will learn to divide fractions. In addition, they will learn how to develop persistence as a habit for problem solving.

Lesson: Review multiplication of fractions. Instruct students in the process of dividing fractions, noting specific differences in the two procedures.

Assignment: Use that skill to solve a picture puzzle.

The purpose of this lesson is to have students experience the sense of accomplishment derived from being persistent toward a goal. Students will persevere to construct an obscure fraction puzzle.

I. Input
A. Establish a personal need for developing a more positive attitude by expressing negativism often heard as students work.

B. Discuss ways to improve performance in school work. Accept student suggestions highlighting key ideas for referral.

C. Ask for a word that means all the things you have written down. (persistence)

D. Redefine persistence in terms given by students.

• Question: "Describe a time when someone you know or have learned about was persistent."

• Question: "Describe a time when *you* were persistent."

• Question: "Why is it important to be persistent?"

II. Process
A. Students are seated in groups of four. Although each student's puzzle in the group is different, the students provide support for each other as they begin to problem solve.

B. Teacher models the problem solving involved.

C. Papers are passed to the students, and general directions are given. Problem solving begins.

• Question: "What was the task you were to complete today?"

• Question: "What were your first thoughts as you were handed the puzzle paper?"

• Question: "How could those thoughts have affected your performance of the task?"

III. Output
• Question: "How many of you were able to complete the assignment? If you are not yet finished, what would it take to complete the puzzle?"

• Question: "Describe the circumstances when you have given up on an assignment before it was finished."

• Question: "What has enabled you to solve your task today?"
Review the definitions of persistence students gave at the beginning of class.

• Question: "How might a person who practices persistence have an advantage over a person who does not?"

• Question: "In using persistence today you were able to solve the puzzle. How might persistence help you outside the classroom?"

The lesson design above is an example of integrating the habits of mind at the elementary level, but the habits must be reinforced continuously throughout instruction at the secondary level for them to become habituated. Students need many opportunities over the years to practice and to learn the habits of mind.

Figure 5.3 contains another example of a lesson design. This lesson comes from Cathy Earl, a math teacher at Danbury High School in Danbury, Texas.

DESIGNING LEARNING TASKS

The teachers in Marcy Open School in Minneapolis, Minnesota, take a somewhat different approach to designing learning tasks. They first lay out the product or assessment, and then they describe the specifics of the task at hand. Finally, they choose which habit of mind would be most appropriate for that content (see Figure 5.4 on p. 71). They can thus attend to the necessary curriculum and, at the same time, focus on the habits of mind. They might take this work to the next level by considering an assessment that would require using the particular habits of mind they chose as a focus.

The examples in this chapter show how habits of mind can easily be integrated into lessons and units of study. If we are serious about changing students' behavior, we must integrate the habits at every opportunity. The adage "What is expected is inspected and will be respected!" captures this need. We are living in a time when content, thinking processes, and habits of mind are all necessary to prepare the workers and citizens society needs to address the complexities of the next century.

FIGURE 5.3
Sample Lesson

Overlapping Triangles–Congruence

Intelligent Behavior Emphasized: Persistence
__X__ Directly Taught _____ Practiced

Content Objective: The learner will apply the triangle congruence theorems to prove angles and segments congruent in overlapping triangles.

Time Frame: This lesson could be taught in two 90-minute blocks or three to four traditional periods.

Teacher Strategies	Student Activities
Explain and model the intelligent behavior framework to help students develop an understanding of persistence. Monitor student groups. Ask students to elaborate and clarify if necessary and then summarize.	In groups of three or four, students work through the intelligent behavior framework. When ready, they display the results of their thinking on chart paper and explain it to the total class.
Hand out copies of overlapping figures from Math Ties Book A1. Tell students to practice the attributes of persistence as they work.	*Think-Pair-Share* Students work independently at first. After about 20 minutes, they pair. Finally, they share with the entire class.
Students complete Metacognitive Strategy. Ask for volunteers to share.	Students complete the Metacognitive Strategy. Students share their metacognition.
Review the triangle congruence theorems previously taught by soliciting them from students.	Students respond to teacher's question.

FIGURE 5.3—*continued*
Sample Lesson

Teacher Strategies	Student Activities
Explain that now we will use these theorems to prove angles and segments of overlapping triangles congruent. Using questioning techniques, lead students to make connections between the persistence and overlapping figures exercises to what we are about to do. Model an example. Put another problem on the overhead. Ask for volunteers to share.	Students listen, take notes, and respond to questions. Students work in pairs to solve the problem. Students share.
Clarify and elaborate as necessary.	
Ask: What attributes of persistence did you find yourself or your partner using?	Students respond.
Assign problems for completion. Monitor, question, and encourage.	Students work alone or in pairs.
Metacognition: Use the Metacognitive Strategy to close and assess the lesson.	Metacognition: Students complete and share the Metacognitive Strategy.

Source: Cathy Earl, math teacher, Danbury High School, Danbury, Texas.

FIGURE 5.4
Student Performance Task

	Check the Intelligent Behaviors Necessary for This Task
Level: Middle **Circle the Appropriate Competencies:** Problem solving Reading Writing Project Other: French reading	
Topic/Title: Trends **Level of Difficulty:** Middle School (first year)	☐ Persistence
Standard: (Check those that apply.) ☐ Complex Thinker ☐ Cooperative Group Member ☐ Information Processor ☐ Effective Communicator	☐ Decreasing impulsivity
Product: Students will form a hypothesis about the clothing they wear and how prepared they are for class as it relates to days of the week and the weather. Using data collected daily in class, groups of students will show average dress and readiness trends, and they will make a prediction about a day in the following week. Other variables will be examined and considered, such as field trips, changes in schedules, and whole-group assemblies. Their findings will be presented to the class.	☐ Listening to others
Description of Task We have kept daily data on the weather, what students wear to class and bring to class, and any change of group routine for that given day. In a group of three to four, you will	☐ Flexibility in thinking
First . . . • Form a hypothesis about what your class has tendencies to do: What kind of weather are we having when students are well-organized? What do they wear when the weather is rainy, sunny, warm, and cool and windy? What color do they wear when the weather is like that (the three examples given)?	☐ Metacognition ☐ Checking for accuracy
Then . . . • Read the task carefully and assign specific duties to each member of your group. Indicate what those were for each of you on the Data Collection Sheet. • Collect the data from the sheets mounted in the front of the room and transfer them to the sheet provided (Data Collection Sheet). • Use a calculator to add and average all data for Monday through Friday. Only use data collected when the weather was as it is described on your Data Collection Sheet. For example, because snow is not mentioned on the sheet, ignore any data taken on snowy days. • Present your findings to the class. Also, share your hypothesis and show whether or not your findings support it.	☐ Questioning ☐ Transferring knowledge
Special Notes: This is a French class. The data collected are in French and will be reported in French. Students must be able to understand the recorded data to process the information. The goal is always to use the language skills one is acquiring while performing complex reasoning and thinking intelligently.	☐ Precision of language ☐ Using all senses
Performance Criteria: A successful group will provide a well thought-out, rational hypothesis and show accurate data and calculation. All group members will participate, fully performing their duties in the group. Presentations will clearly communicate the group's findings and show full participation. (For Rubrics: see Marcy Open School Problem Solving and the ACTFL guidelines: Novice Low-Mid).	☐ Creativity
Task Designer: Camilla Grahn Date: July 1994	☐ Curiosity

Source: Teachers in Marcy Open School, Minneapolis, Minnesota.

6

Teaching the Habits of Mind Directly

Arthur L. Costa and Bena Kallick

A great pleasure in life is doing what people say you cannot do.

Tommy John

The habits of mind don't readily lend themselves to instructional "recipes." Still, many educators have developed strategies for teaching the habits of mind directly, from building students' awareness of them to instructing children specifically on each habit. These educators share some of their strategies in this chapter. Though their processes and methods differ, all of their work has a common strain: Effective teachers are always alert for and seize opportunities to engage, reinforce, illuminate, and practice the habits of mind.

BUILDING AWARENESS

Many teachers build students' awareness of the habits of mind through the questions they pose. For example, before you begin a learning activity, ask questions that cue students about and focus their attention on the importance and use of one or more of the habits. For example, you might ask

- "As you anticipate your projects, which of the habits of mind might we need to use?"
- "In working these math problems, which of the habits of mind will help us?"

• "As we read, which of the habits of mind will we use to help understand the story?"

After a learning activity, pose questions that lead to reflection on and synthesis of the habits of mind:

• "As you reflect on your work on this project, which of the habits of mind did you find yourself using?"
• "As you solved these problems, which of the habits of mind did you use?"
• "As you worked in groups to design a plan, what metacognitive strategies did you use to monitor your performance of the habits of mind?"

Well-constructed questions also cue students to transfer and apply the habits of mind to situations different from those in which the habits were learned. For example,

• "In what other classes might you use these habits of mind?"
• "In what other situations in your life would your use of these habits of mind be beneficial?"
• "In what careers or professions would people have to draw forth these habits of mind?"

Other intriguing questions can be posed to stimulate discussion of the habits of mind:

• "How might an intelligent person use the habits of mind to choose a doctor?"
• "How would the habits of mind be used in purchasing an automobile?"
• "Which of the habits of mind would be helpful in intelligently reading a newspaper (or watching television)?"

TEACHING THE HABITS DIRECTLY

Many teachers have developed powerful strategies for teaching the habits of mind directly. Though some of these strategies focus on one habit, other habits are often interdependently linked to them. In fact, clusters of habits can be taught, depending on student needs, the context and content of the lesson, and the school's educational priorities.

The following examples are drawn from many different classrooms. We have tried to provide some rich exemplars for you to use as a model for your own teaching. You will, of course, want to draw on your own skills and repertoire and add to this list.

Persisting

If the only tool you have is a hammer, you will treat the whole world as if it were a nail.

Edward de Bono

When students approach a problem, they often have the misconception that there is "one best strategy." Once that strategy does not work, they give up in frustration. People persist because they can draw on multiple ways to solve problems. If "Plan A" doesn't work, they back up and try "Plan B." Therefore, teachers must celebrate multiple ways of finding solutions: "Isn't that wonderful! We've found four different ways of solving this problem!"

It is better to teach students three ways to solve one problem than it is to teach them one way to solve three problems. We've seen many teachers who are in the habit of asking, "Who has another way to solve this problem?" "What is another approach to solving this problem?" or "What are some other strategies?" They then ask students to write about their many different strategies for a "strategy box." When students are in doubt about another problem, they can refer to their strategy box! As students build their repertoire of strategies, they also begin to see the merit of working with a diverse number of students.

Teaching persistence is a matter of teaching strategy. Persistence does not just mean working to get it right. Persistence means knowing that getting stuck is a cue to "try something else."

MANAGING IMPULSIVITY

The secret of getting ahead is getting started. The secret of getting started is breaking your complex overwhelming tasks into small manageable tasks, and then starting on the first one.

Mark Twain

Before any learning activity, teachers must take the time to develop and discuss strategies for attacking problems. Such work should include rules, directions, time constraints, and purposes. Students can use this guidance during their work and to evaluate their performance afterwards.

During an activity, teachers should invite students to share their progress, thought processes, and perceptions of their own behavior. Guide students through metacognition by asking them to describe where they are in using a particular strategy and to reflect on how well that strategy is working. At this time, it is also useful to ask students to map their progress visually. They can describe the trail of thinking to this point in their work. Then they can describe the paths they intend to pursue next to solve their problem.

This kind of visual map also serves as a diagnostic cognitive map of student thinking, which the teacher can use to give more individualized assistance. If students are using a time management plan, this is a good point for them to review and revise their plan. This also is an excellent time to provide students with peer coaching or to introduce the concept of a critical friend (Costa & Kallick, 1995).

Once the learning activity is completed, teachers can invite students to evaluate how they worked with the rules, strategies, and instructions. Students can use this reflection to generate alternative, more efficient strategies to be used in the future.

We know a kindergarten teacher who begins and ends each day with a class meeting. In the morning, children plan for the day. They decide what learning tasks to accomplish and how to accomplish them. They allocate classroom space, assign roles, and develop criteria for appropriate conduct. Throughout the day, the teacher calls attention to plans and ground rules established during the morning. The teacher also invites students to compare what they are doing with what was agreed. Then, before dismissal, students hold another class meeting to reflect on, evaluate, and plan further strategies and criteria.

Wait time is another important element in learning to manage impulsivity. When using wait time, teachers will want to share with students why they ask questions and then remain silent. Tell children that you are looking for thoughtful, reflective answers, and you will wait a minute or so before calling on anyone. Let them know you are not looking for how quickly someone answers a question, and you will not be impressed with answers that are shouted out or hands that shoot up before the question is asked completely.

In one school, everyone was working on the goal of using wait time. The principal stopped a student running down the hallway, pulled out a stopwatch, and showed the student the timing of one minute. Then the principal asked, "Can you tell me why you were running?" Stopwatches, egg timers, and other timing devices help students learn how to wait appropriately. Figure 6.1 shows how letter writing can be a useful way for students to reflect on the habits of mind and learn to manage their impulsivity.

LISTENING WITH UNDERSTANDING AND EMPATHY

Nothing increases the respect and gratitude of one man for another more than when he is heard exactly and with interest.

R. Umbach

I understand that when I'm reading a question I listen for key words to help me go about understanding the question and help me answer it.

Friendship Valley Student Self-Assessment
Friend Valley Elementary School
Carroll County, Maryland

Interestingly, we spend about 55 percent of our lives listening, but listening is one of the least taught skills in schools. Adults often say they are listening when actually they are rehearsing in their heads what they will say when it's their turn to speak. We need to teach students the skills of listening: paraphrasing, questioning, and taking turns talking.

Effective listeners set aside certain unproductive mental patterns that may block their capacity to listen. When we listen, we often are fighting the urge to do one of several things:

FIGURE 6.1
A 3rd Grader's Reflections on the Habits of Mind

Dear Ms. —

Hello.... We were estimating the cost of our school supplies. Then we calculated the prices of the supplies. The cost of everything together was nineteen sixty [$19.60]. Most of the groups got different numbers for the estimates.

I used intelligent behaviors [habits of mind]. The first one I used was persistence. The second one I used was prior knowledge. I used persistence because I needed to keep trying to get the right answer. I used prior knowledge because I had to use what I know about money. That's all I have to say.

Sincerely,
(Student)

- *Compare.* When our mind compares, we are distracted from listening because we try to assess who is smarter, more competent, or more resourceful.
- *Read Minds.* When we read minds, we try to figure out what the other person really is thinking and feeling. We don't pay much attention to what our partner is saying.
- *Rehearse.* When our attention is on preparing and crafting our next comment, we don't take time to listen.
- *Filter.* When we listen to some things and not to others, we pay attention only to those ideas with which we agree or disagree.
- *Judge.* The negative labels we hold about others or their ideas prejudice our listening. We don't pay as much attention to what they say because we've already decided they are unqualified or unworthy.
- *Dream.* When we are only half listening, something the person says suddenly triggers a chain of private associations. Then we're off and running in our own fantasy world.
- *Identify.* Autobiographical thinking blocks our listening because we relate what the other person says to our own experience. For example, a friend describes a visit to the automobile repair shop, which reminds me of my car's most recent breakdown.
- *Give Advice.* Because we view ourselves as great problem solvers, ready with help and eager to give suggestions, we immediately begin searching for the right solution to the other person's problem.
- *Argue.* When we argue, counter, or debate, other people may feel that they've not been heard because we're so quick to disagree.
- *Be Right.* Because our mind is made up, we twist facts, raise our voice, make excuses, accuse others, or call up past sins to avoid being wrong.
- *Derail.* When we are bored or uncomfortable with the topic, we change the subject or deflect the conversation to another issue.
- *Placate.* Because we want to be amiable and have people like us, we agree with everything to avoid confrontation.
- *Scrutinize.* Asking repeated, probing questions drags the conversation into a hole of analytical minutiae and may cause others to lose sight of larger issues.

To practice the skills of listening, ask students to paraphrase what another student has said before they add to what was said or offer their own comments. Invite students to describe what goes on in their heads as they listen. For example, you might ask, "As your partner was speaking, what metacognitive processes did you use to manage, monitor, and modify your listening capacities when you had an urge to. . .?" Figure 6.2 shows a poster one teacher at Friendship Valley School in Westminster, Maryland, uses to remind her students of good listening habits.

FIGURE 6.2
Listening Poster

Distractors to Listening

Strategies for Students to Manage Distractors to Listening

Before I start to think:

- **What are my distractions?**
- **What will I do to stay focused?**

Distraction: Anything that pulls your attention from what you should be doing—listening, reading, writing, and sharing

Class Brainstorming of Distractions

What I see or hear:

- **Pictures on the wall**
- **Noises in the hall**
- **Children talking**
- **Teacher talking**

- **Lawn mower outside**
- **Noises in the classroom**
- **Chairs moving**
- **Books**

The room may be:

Too hot	Too cold	Can't see	Too sunny
Too noisy	Can't hear	Too many things going on	

Source: Teacher at Friendship Valley Elementary School, Carroll County, Maryland.

THINKING FLEXIBLY

We need people who can read and write. But what we really need is people who cannot only read the instructions but change them. They need to be able to think outside the lines.

Richard Gurin, CEO and President
Binney & Smith Crayola Products

We enhance the habit of thinking flexibly when we must alter our perspective and see things from other points of view. Macro-centric thinking means seeing the big picture. Micro-centric means finding the details. Retro-centric means starting with the end point and working backward toward the beginning. To help students understand these different perspectives, have them read stories such as *The True Story of the Three Little Pigs from the Wolf's Point of View* or Chris Van Allsburg's *Two Bad Ants*. Deliberately place students in groups because of their different learning styles, which will help them understand and appreciate varying points of view. Create a problem-solving team with students who have visual strengths and students whose style is auditory. Ask them to explain to each other how to solve a problem "outside" their best learning style.

You can take this approach even further by giving students problems in which they have to change their perspective to find an answer. Have them describe how they had to look at the problem differently and where else in life a change in perspective would be important. For example, can you find the pattern in this string of letters?

AEFHIKLMNTVWXYZ

THINKING ABOUT THINKING (METACOGNITION)

Thinking Aloud . . . Allowed!

Sometimes teachers are so anxious for students to find correct answers that they omit discussions of the processes, strategies, and steps that produce the answer. Asking students to describe their thinking while they solve a problem seems to beget even more thinking. Students must do more than learn how to find answers; they must become aware of the cognitive processes that produced the answer.

Some teachers ask students to keep a running record of their thought processes as they solve a problem. This record is a powerful teaching tool. It can reveal to you that the student is not accomplishing what was intended because the student is unaware of an unsuccessful strategy. Once you know this problem, you can teach another strategy.

Teachers also use questioning strategies to clarify students' problem-solving processes: "Jeff, you figured out that the answer was 44; Jody says the answer is 33. Let's hear how you came up with 44. Retrace your steps for us." Generating alternative strategies for solving problems and posting them around the room serves two purposes: (1) Students are surrounded by multiple possibilities for problem solving when they are stuck, and (2) students see that there is no single best way of doing things.

Clarifying helps students to reexamine their own problem-solving processes, to identify their own errors, and to self-correct. The teacher might ask, "How much is 3 plus 4?"

The student replies, "The answer is 12."

Rather than correct the student, the teacher clarifies: "Gary, how did you arrive at that answer?"

Gary answers, "Well, I multiplied 4 and 3 and got . . . oh, I see! I multiplied instead of added."

By clarifying, the teacher causes the student to return to his or her thinking processes. By restating the processes, students "hear themselves" and become self-correcting.

Teachers also can ask students to identify what they have done well and invite them to seek feedback from their peers. For example, the teacher might ask, "What have you done that you're proud of?" This kind of question helps students become more conscious of their own behavior, and they learn to apply a set of internal criteria for behavior they consider "good" (Costa, 1991).

When students reflect on their learning, teachers can guide that reflection to be metacognitive. Many teachers ask students to solve a problem and then describe their steps to someone else, using these guidelines:

1. What did you do first?
2. What steps did you take when you were uncertain about your work?
3. How did you change your course of action? Was it profitable?
4. If you were to do this work again, is there anything that you would do differently? If so, describe what that might be and why you would do it.

Tell students that answers such as "I can't" or "I don't know how to" are unacceptable. Instead, they should identify what information is required, what materials are needed, or what skills are lacking in order for them to resolve a situation. This reflection helps students identify the boundaries between what they know and what they need to know. Reflection also develops a persevering attitude and enhances the student's ability to create strategies that will produce needed data.

Eventually, the processes of thinking and problem solving become the subjects of classroom discussion. Because teachers realize that the intent of metacognitive dialogue is not to arrive at closure, they use techniques and strategies to maintain "opensure"—continuing engagement of the thinking processes. A variety of strategies can help you engage and sustain this metacognition.

When you want students to check for accuracy, ask these questions:

- "How do you know you are right?"
- "What other ways can you prove that you are correct?"

Pause and clarify during your conversation, but don't interrupt:

- "What did you do first?"
- "What clues did you have that you were on the right track?"
- "How did you know where to begin?"
- "What led you to make that decision?"
- "When you said you started at the beginning, how did you know where to begin?"

Provide students with data, but not answers:

- "I think you heard it wrong. Let me repeat the question."
- "You need to check your addition."

Resist making value judgments or agreeing with students' answers:

- "So, your answer is 48. Who came up with a different answer?"
- "That's one possibility. Who solved it another way?"

Stay focused on thinking processes:

- "Tell us what strategies you used to solve the problem."
- "What steps did you take in your solution?"

Invite overt verbalization of thinking processes, and encourage persistence:

- "Tell us what's going on inside your head."
- "C'mon, you can do it! Hang in there."

STRIVING FOR ACCURACY

It's hard to wring my hands when I am busy rolling up my sleeves.

Linda Geraci

Sally Ride used [the habit of mind] checking for accuracy in the spaceship Challenger!

Student response to Thommie DePinto Piercy
Friendship Valley School
Westminster, Maryland

Students must come to see that striving for accuracy is of great value not only in the classroom but in the world as well. Pharmaceutical research, surgery, piloting, bookkeeping—all require a commitment to accuracy. Sometimes teachers take home stacks of student papers to correct, placing ticks and check marks to indicate correct or incorrect answers. In this process, teachers get a lot of practice checking for accuracy and precision, but they rob students of the opportunity to check for themselves. Consider this alternative: Simply write on the top of the paper, "You have three errors on this page." Now it is the student's responsibility to find and correct the mistakes, not the teacher's.

Another useful strategy is "three before me." No paper should be turned in to the teacher without being checked at least three times. Organize students into teams of four so that they have three other people to share responsibility for striving for accuracy.

QUESTIONING AND POSING PROBLEMS

It is in the formulation of the problem that individuality is expressed, that creativity is stimulated, that nuances and subtleties are discovered.

Herbert Thelen

Whatever the subject area, it is helpful for students to pose study questions for themselves before and during their reading of textual material. Self-generating questions facilitate comprehension. We know that reading with a purpose stimulates a more focused mind. Questioning while reading provides an opportunity for the reader to predict what is coming next in the story. Many students find it useful to keep their questions in a response log or reading log. Then they can begin to answer the questions raised as they reflect on the reading and seek other sources.

Invite students to compose questions to be used in a study guide or on a test. For example, ask students to read the "Three-Story Intellect" vignette from Chapter 3. Then ask them to compose three first-story, second-story, and third-story questions for the teacher to use in constructing a quiz or test. Some teachers ask students to prepare questions in a group to be given to another group. The second group then answers the questions, and the first group evaluates those answers along with the original questions. This activity serves two important purposes. First, students ask more difficult questions because they want to make them hard for the other group. Second, they must be able to answer their own questions, which challenges their own thinking as well.

Sometimes the most significant questions are generated through the research process. As demonstrated in Chapter 3, there are many ways to guide students to generate powerful questions worthy of research. In addition, students can learn that a thoughtful way to end their research paper is with a set of questions generated as a result of their inquiry. Students gain much when they realize that there is always more to know!

Applying Past Knowledge to New Situations

The main fuel to speed the world's progress is our stock of knowledge, and the brake is our lack of imagination.

Julian Simon

Teachers must take time to both scaffold and bridge new learning. Scaffolding means building a knowledge structure by going back into previous information and drawing it forth. The recalled information then serves as a framework for incorporating new information.

Think of building a new stage in an auditorium. The scaffolds are the structures that hold up the stage as it is being built. Once the structure is complete, however, it is expected to stand on its own, without the scaffolds. Thus it is with learning. Students need scaffolds to support them through new learning. Then they must take the new learning and test its viability as an independent structure. Finally, they must be able to bridge, or transfer, that learning to other situations in their lives inside and outside school.

For example, whenever you begin a new learning, pose questions that will cause students to search their memories to brainstorm and generate past knowledge:

- "What do you remember about . . . ?"
- "When have you ever seen anything like this?"
- "As you recall . . . ."
- "Tell what you know about . . . ."

When the lesson is over, always ask students to apply their knowledge to the future:

- "If you were to design a new . . . ?"
- "What would it be like if . . . ?"
- "Where else would you use this information?"
- "In what other situations could you apply this?"

The intent of scaffolding and bridging is to help students get into the habit of drawing forth previous knowledge and applying it to new and novel situations.

THINKING AND COMMUNICATING WITH CLARITY AND PRECISION

This report, by its very length, defends itself against the risk of being read.
Winston Churchill

Many times, students' and adults' oral language is filled with omissions, generalizations, and vagueness. Our language is conceptual rather than operational, value laden, and sometimes deceiving (Costa & Marzano, 1991). Being alert to this vagueness and then clarifying or probing for specificity causes others to define their terms, become specific about their actions, make precise comparisons, and use accurate descriptors (Laborde, 1984). Clarifying language also clarifies thoughts.

The vague terms we use fall into several categories:

- *Universals:* always, never, all, or everybody.
- *Vague action verbs:* know about, understand, appreciate.
- *Comparators:* better, newer, cheaper, more.
- *Unreferenced pronouns:* they, them, we.
- *Unspecified groups:* teachers, parents, things.
- *Assumed rules or traditions:* ought, should, or must.

When you hear or see such words or phrases in students' speech or writing, ask them to specify, define, or reference their terms. For example,

When you hear:	Clarify by probing for specificity:
"He NEVER listens to me."	"Never?" or "Never ever?"
"Everybody has one."	"Everybody?" or "Who, exactly?"
"THINGS go better with . . . ."	"Which things specifically?"
"Things GO better with . . . ."	"Go? Go how, specifically?"
"Things go BETTER with . . . ."	"Better than what?"
"You SHOULDN'T do that!"	"What would happen if you did?"
"The PARENTS . . . ."	"Which parents?"
"I want them to UNDERSTAND."	"What exactly will they be doing if they understand?"
"This cereal is MORE NUTRITIOUS."	"More nutritious than what?"
"THEY won't let me!"	"Who is 'they'?"
"The teachers . . . ."	"Which teachers?"
"I want him to be nice."	"Nice? How specifically should he be nice?"

Critical thinkers are characterized by their ability to use specific terminology, to refrain from overgeneralizations, and to support their assumptions with valid data. Clarifying and probing by having students use precise language develop those characteristics (Ennis, 1985).

GATHERING DATA THROUGH ALL SENSES

By pushing the right biological buttons in the brain, scientists have found they can make the future brighter for many children whose development otherwise would have been stunted. How the buttons work is perhaps the most amazing thing of all. The buttons are the senses: vision, taste, smell, touch, and sound and they can be pushed by experiences from the outside world.

R. Kotulak

When our senses are dull and sluggish, our thinking is dull and sluggish. Because all information gets into the head through our sensory pathways, teachers will want to plan lessons that engage as many of the senses as possible. For example, "In this lesson, how can I maximize opportunities to visualize, listen, experience, move, smell, taste, touch, and feel?" The more senses that are engaged, the greater the learning.

Sensory exercises hone our powers of perception. For example,

• *Sight.* Ninety percent of our sensory input comes through our eyes. To improve peripheral vision, ask students to shift their eyes from right to left several times as fast as they can without moving their head. Have them try to focus on 10 different objects in 10 seconds by scanning the room. Can they name the objects in the order in which they saw them?

• *Touch.* Our largest sense organ is our skin. With their eyes closed, have students feel various textured objects: sandpaper, cotton, silk, steel. Ask them to describe what they are feeling as they feel it.

• *Sound.* While we can't improve our hearing, we can improve our listening. Have students close their eyes and listen to a single sound. This exercise will require them to shut out extraneous noise. For example, as they listen to music, ask them to single out one instrument to follow (like the bass guitar or the violin).

• *Smell.* Provide students with various fragrances: perfume, cinnamon, cloves, wintergreen, and eucalyptus. Have them describe what they are smelling. Have them take several small sniffs rather than sniff deeply. Instruct them to keep their mouths open as they smell. If they draw the scent into the mouth, it gives an extra dimension to the smell.

• *Taste.* Humans taste four basic flavors: sweet, sour, salty, and bitter. With the students' eyes closed, place a sample of each taste on their tongue: sugar, salt, lemon juice, and vinegar. Have students describe what they taste. Between tastes, cleanse the palate with crackers, bread, or water.

CREATING, IMAGINING, INNOVATING

I believe everybody is creative, and everybody is talented. I just don't think that everybody is disciplined. I think that's a rare commodity.

Al Hirschfield

This extended excerpt from the classroom of Lisa Davis, a teacher in West Orchard Elementary School in Chappaqua, New York, provides a rich example of encouraging ingenuity, originality, and insightfulness:

As my colleagues and I were discussing the literal interpretations many of my students had written about a poem I asked them to reflect on, we began discussing how hard it is to teach someone to think abstractly. Later, as I was thinking back to that conversation, I thought of a comment my friend Raina makes whenever I'm being inflexible. She says, "Lisa, can you please get outside of the box!" That was it! I needed to get my kids to think outside of the box.

The next morning, I put up a slide on the monitor that said, "Think Outside the Box!" Immediately children started to question what I meant. Then I said, "Let me read some examples from last night's homework and you tell me if the person was 'in the box'—which means they were thinking literally—or 'out of the box'—which would mean they were thinking abstractly."

I reread the poem "Alice" by Shel Silverstein and some of the students' written reflections. It was obvious who was "getting" the meaning of literal and abstract and who wasn't. Suddenly, Anna connected it to an activity we did the first week of school. She said, "This is like the survival kit you gave us on the first day of school. You gave us a rubber band, not so we could band our papers together but to remind us to be flexible in our thinking or to stretch our ideas."

James chimed in, "Oh yeah. Remember, I thought the button was to keep in case a button came off my shirt. And then someone told me that was too obvious so we switched it to: Remember to button your lips if you have something mean to say or you could use it to button your ideas together—to make connections."

Soon kids were reminding me of other examples from the survival kit. "Yes, yes, yes!" I exclaimed. "Now you're getting it!" My excitement had me jumping in and out of an imaginary box. Then I said, "It's like onions and math!"

Huh? My students looked at me bewildered. It was if we were all headed in the same direction, and then I decided to switch tracks. Determined—and a firm believer in wait time—I waited. And waited. Finally, Amy said, "They can both make you cry!"

"Yes!" I exclaimed. "How else are onions and math connected?"

Don yelled out, "You can cut the onion into rings and make a Venn diagram out of them."

Laura whispered, "He's in the box."

I offered: "What a great thought Don, but that is kind of literal because we could actually cut an onion in rings. Keep thinking." Then Beth spoke.

The room got respectfully quiet as we all turned to look at Beth, a special needs child who rarely speaks unless she is absolutely confident that she has a "right" answer. She said, "It's like when you plant onions."

"Okay," I encouraged. "Keep going, Beth. Help us see what you're thinking."

"You plant the baby onion in the dirt and it grows," she stated as if the connection was obvious.

"How is that related to math?" I probed for further understanding.

"Well, when you plant the small onion in the ground, it grows. And when you add small numbers together, they grow!"

"Oh, wow, Beth!" I exclaimed. "That is very divergent thinking! Class, is she in the box or out of the box?"

The whole class chimed, "Out of the box!"

The discussion was so powerful that I had to capitalize on the enthusiasm by extending the lesson. When the kids went to the gym, I headed to the kindergarten classroom to borrow the "junk boxes" that they use for sorting. I randomly mixed objects, placing a pile in the middle of each table. When the children returned, I explained that they needed to discuss various attributes of the materials and then sort them—keeping in mind the discussion we had in the morning regarding literal and abstract thinking.

As I circulated, I realized that nearly every table was sorting by the obvious attributes (bikes in one pile, keys in another). I began to ask, "Are you in the box or out of the box?" Some tables rearranged their materials; others stuck with their first ideas.

Whenever I do an activity like this, I do a "three-minute check-in": Kids at one table can ask kids at other tables questions to get ideas or to clarify the task. Martin clarified that the task was to sort the objects in a way that wouldn't be obvious to the rest of us. (I have found this strategy to be very beneficial because it takes the onus off me as the only one with the ability to solve problems, and it also requires children to interpret what I've said and explain it in a different way.)

As we circulated from table to table, we had fun trying to figure out how each table sorted its objects. When we got to one table, we were stumped. They had sorted their objects into two piles. One had baseball cards and shells, while the other had keys, buttons, and rocks. Finally, someone yelled out, "Fragile and hard!"

A member of the table confirmed the answer by saying, "We actually named the groups destructible and indestructible with human hands."

As we approached another table where all the items still were mixed together, I impulsively said, "You were supposed to leave your objects in their *sorted* piles!"

Jeremy reminded me to be patient: "We did. They all fit in one category."

Sixteen kids and I stared at the pile of bikes, bugs, keys, cars, and pasta wheels. After many guesses, the table members had to tell us what they were thinking: "The keys are used to start the car, the pasta wheels are in case of a flat, the bugs splat onto the windshield, and the bikes go on the roof when you want to go to the trail to go bike riding. All the items relate to a car!" Now that's getting outside the box!

Students need help knowing how to tap their reservoir of originality and liberate their creative potentials. Techniques such as brainstorming, Mind Mapping®, and metaphorical thinking help to loosen thinking. For example, ask a student to describe in what way gravity is like a feather. How does the Escher drawing of people moving up and down the stairs serve as a perfect interpretation for *Romeo and Juliet?* Create your own plant and an environment in which it can live. (For further suggestions, refer to such authors as Treffinger & Nassab, 2000; Treffinger & Nassab, 1998; Parnes, 1991; and Gordon, 1961.)

Asking students to find similarities and differences in two or more unlike objects helps them make new connections and find hidden relationships:

- "How does it feel to be a flat tire?"
- "How do you think a zero feels?"
- "Which is crisper: celery or yellow?"
- "Which is the happiest room in your house?

Incorporating such generative questioning as an integral part of any subject matter helps students learn how to initiate creative thought when a situation demands it.

RESPONDING WITH WONDERMENT AND AWE

Good teachers are passionate about ideas, learning, and their relationship with students. . . . These teachers did more than teach to set standards or use approved techniques. Their classroom relationships featured "interest, enthusiasm, inquiry, excitement, discovery, risk taking, and fun." Their cognitive scaffolding of concepts and teaching strategies was "held together with emotional bonds."

P. Woods and B. Jeffrey, *Teachable Moments*

Recently, a Dutch psychologist tried to figure out what separated chess masters and chess grand masters. He subjected groups of each to a battery of tests: IQ, memory, and spatial reasoning. He found no testing difference between them. In the end, the only difference he found was this: Grand masters simply loved chess more. They had more passion and commitment to it. Passion may be the key to creativity (Thornton, 1999).

Enrapture students with awesome phenomena, intriguing situations, and jaw-dropping experiments. Surround them with beautiful scenes, technological marvels, and science fiction. Let their imaginations take flight! What is important about the learning is not so much the content as the enjoyment, enthusiasm, and fascination that students experience about the content. Allow them free range to explore whatever they are intrigued with—as long as they are experiencing the passion.

Invite students to share their interests. What electrifies and mystifies them? In a safe environment, students will feel free to share their fascination, their emotions, and their exhilaration. Make it cool to be passionate about something! Stay with a learning over time, not because the curriculum calls for it but because students have sustained interest in it. Time your lessons so that solutions to problems are not found by the time the bell rings. Instead, allow students to carry their curiosity, ambiguity, and uncertainties over until the next day or class period.

This habit of mind is probably more caught than taught. Make your lessons lively and animated. Share with your students your fascinations with your content; allow them to see you enthralled and excited about a problem or discovery and fascinated with your own craft of teaching.

TAKING RESPONSIBLE RISKS

Only those who will risk going too far can possibly find out how far one can go.

T. S. Eliot

Students will be more inclined to take risks in an environment that is safe; free from judgment; and accepting of all ideas, human differences, and points of view. Invite students to find examples of risk taking and analyze and report on it. They can look in the fields of athletics (Richard Fosbury), politics (Nelson Mandela), technology (Bill Gates), entertainment (D. W. Griffith), science (Galileo), the arts (Vincent van Gogh), business (J. P. Morgan)—the possibilities are endless.

What was the nature of the risks these people took? Were the risks calculated or spontaneous? What constitutes the differences between calculated and spontaneous risks? Which risks paid off, which did not, and why? Invite students to compare risk taking in various fields: artistic risk taking versus risk taking in space exploration, for example. Which is riskier and why? Which was riskier: Columbus's voyage or Neil Armstrong's? Why?

Read stories and report on adventurers in space, explorers of new lands, social activists, research pioneers, inventors, and artists who were called "cutting edge." Describe their characteristics and the conditions in which they took the risks.

Invite students to describe risks they have taken and the results. When is it appropriate or inappropriate to take a risk? What clues should inform your decision to take risks?

Consider creating a "risk taker's park." Tell students: "We are going to design a new park for risk takers. We will erect five statues dedicated to the greatest risk takers in history in five different fields: social/political, visual/artistic, logical/mathematical, athletic, and literary." Have students work in teams to decide who they want to place in the park and why. Students can also design the park and write letters to the town council or board of supervisors describing why they believe such a park should be built.

FINDING HUMOR

If you can laugh at it, you can live with it.

Erma Bombeck

Teachers need to build humor into the classroom environment. Create a bulletin board to post funny cartoons, witty sayings, silly pictures, and photos. Let students update the space as they find and contribute new items.

Develop humor-building rituals. Read comics and cartoons together. Encourage students to cut out, bring to school, and share comics they find especially funny. Agree to watch comedies on television, and ask students to share what made them laugh and what they thought were the most hilarious sequences. Make an album of favorite jokes, cartoons, and sayings. Encourage students to develop their own comic vision and to look for humor in daily life. At the end of the day, ask students to name at least one funny thing they saw or heard that day. Then they can draw a picture that illustrates the funny scene.

THINKING INTERDEPENDENTLY

It is good to rub and polish our brain against that of others.

Michael De Montaigne

Working in cooperative groups provides the context for learning many other habits of mind. One cannot work with others without the skills of thinking flexibly, listening with understanding and empathy, thinking about thinking (metacognition), thinking and communicating with clarity and precision, and finding humor.

To ensure that students experience positive interdependence, teachers need to structure cooperative learning situations in which children learn the content *and* are responsible for ensuring that all group members succeed in the assigned task. The learning task must be structured to be cooperative and reciprocal. Each member can succeed individually only if all members succeed collectively.

Purposely structure groups heterogeneously to supply a rich mixture of cultures, languages, styles, modalities, points of view, and levels of development. As they resolve their differences, students must engage and practice the habits of mind. Set standards for effective group work before the work is assigned, then have students monitor their own and each other's contributions.

After the cooperative task is completed, take time to reflect on how well individuals and groups worked together. What contributed to the group's success? How did each group member contribute to and learn from the experience? Encourage students to give nonjudgmental feedback to each other about their observations. (For further elaboration and suggested activities for learning interdependence, see Johnson & Johnson, 1994; O'Leary & Dishon, 1998; and Kagan, 1994.) A student's poster (see Figure 6.3) simply summarizes the benefits of thinking interdependently.

FIGURE 6.3
Student Poster

REMAINING OPEN TO CONTINUOUS LEARNING

The only thing that we can know is that we know nothing and that is the highest flight of human wisdom.

Leo Tolstoy

There can be no such thing as a mistake; we only learn from experience. In a trusting environment, students reflect on their learnings, analyze their experiences, and apply and transfer learnings to new situations. Probably the most powerful strategy for teaching the habit of remaining open to continuous learning is modeling.

Admit to students that you still are learning about the content, about teaching and learning, about the school as a community, and about them as learners. Share your lesson goals and outcomes with students, and describe your instructional strategies and assessment techniques. Then, at the end of the lesson or unit, invite their feedback about what worked and what didn't.

Demonstrate your own humility through self-modification. Express the learnings you have derived from their feedback about your lesson design and instructional effectiveness. Then, let students see you modify your own behavior based upon your learnings.

You might also ask your students to read about or interview corporate leaders, artists, athletes, and remarkable people who are achieving mastery in their craft (Ames, 1997). What are some indicators that those who have achieved mastery never stop learning? Are they ever complacent about their accomplishments? Or do they reflect George Bernard Shaw's belief that men are wise, not in proportion to their experience but in proportion to their capacity for experience?

REFERENCES

Ames, J. E. (1997). *Mastery: Interviews with 30 remarkable people*. Portland, OR: Rudra Press.

Costa, A. (1991). Mediating the metacognitive. In A. Costa (Ed.), *Developing minds: A resource book for teaching thinking* (Rev. ed., Vol. 1, pp. 211–214). Alexandria, VA: Association for Supervision and Curriculum Development.

Costa, A., & Kallick, B. (1995). *Assessment in the learning organization: Shifting the paradigm*. Alexandria, VA: Association for Supervision and Curriculum Development.

Costa, A., & Marzano, R. (1991). Teaching the language of thinking. In A. Costa (Ed.), *Developing minds: A resource book for teaching thinking* (Rev. ed., Vol. 1, pp. 251–254). Alexandria, VA: Association for Supervision and Curriculum Development.

Ennis, R. (1985). Goals for a critical thinking curriculum. In A. Costa (Ed.), *Developing minds: A resource book for teaching thinking* (pp. 54–57). Alexandria, VA: Association for Supervision and Curriculum Development.

Gordon, W. (1961). Synectics: *The development of creative capacity*. New York: Grollier.

Johnson, R., & Johnson, D. (1994). *Learning together and alone: cooperation, competition and individualization*. Needham Heights, MA: Allyn and Bacon.

Kagan, S. (1994). *Cooperative learning*. San Juan Capistrano, CA: Kagan's Cooperative Learning Company.

Laborde, G. (1984). *Influencing with integrity*. Palo Alto, CA: Syntony Press.

O'Leary, P., & Dishon, D. (1998). *Guidebook for cooperative learning*. Holmes Beach, FL: Learning Publications.

Parnes, S. (1991). Creative problem solving. In A. Costa (Ed.), *Developing minds: Programs for teaching thinking* (Rev. Ed., Vol. 2, pp. 54–56). Alexandria, VA: Association for Supervision and Curriculum Development.

Thornton, J. (1999, January 1–3). Getting inside your head. *Honolulu Advertiser, U.S.A. Weekend Magazine*, pp. 8–9.

Treffinger, D. J., & Nassab, C. A. (1998). *Thinking tool guides*. Sarasota, FL: Center for Creative Learning.

Treffinger, D. J., & Nassab, C. A. (2000). *Thinking tool lessons*. Waco, TX: Prufrock Press.

7

USING HABITS OF MIND TO LOOK "INSIDE THE TEXT"

KATHLEEN C. REILLY

Secondary school English departments often strain at the seams from the weight of covering so much material. They are called upon to strengthen grammar basics, promote the importance of spelling, reinforce punctuation rules, and guide students in the purposeful study of literature. These many responsibilities weighed on my mind when I decided to integrate habits of mind with the study of literature and writing in my 12th grade classroom. All the signs indicated that bad things could happen to a good idea if I allowed it to get lost among all the other demands on my time!

Even though my teaching days already were overloaded, I was drawn to research about critical thinking methods. Adolescence is mysterious, for sure, and I had decided that although all my students *could* experience high-level thinking, they simply were not disposed to do it. When I began to introduce thinking skills, students tenaciously expressed the belief that thinking critically was a "natural" gift. In many cases, even those who saw themselves as "good students" felt the process beyond their skills. I was driven by the question of why my students resisted problem solving and decision making.

THE FIRST YEAR

When I first introduced thinking skills to my students, I announced that we were going to use a metaphor as a way to "look inside" the texts we were studying. We started with an exercise on metaphors that we live by, then easily moved into a search for metaphors in the texts we studied. Most interesting, I think, were student responses to my questions about specific metaphors to describe our classroom. They immediately mentioned the placement of my desk in the back of the room, and they told me confidently that ours was a "student-centered classroom." They extended this metaphor when they noted my selection of seminar tables instead of desks to encourage collaboration. They also noted the way I sat in different places among them, not in front of them.

Many other classroom elements served as metaphors for my students. For example, they saw the quotations hanging on the walls as metaphors for my expectations. They were particularly drawn to an Annie Dillard passage: "Why are we reading—if not in hopes of beauty laid bare and life's darkest mysteries probed?" They also pointed to Hannah Arendt's words: "Welcome to a place of excellence . . . where we come together to be the best we can be." Other elements suggested some serious work that would remain after they left the classroom: individual portfolios, dialectic notebooks along the window shelves, and favorite childhood drawings that prompted an early writing assignment.

REFINING MY TEACHING

When that year of metaphor ended, I wanted to get involved further with ways to teach critical thinking. This curiosity led to another academic year of refining my teaching for thinking and discovering ways that students could learn and apply methods. Building on my work with Bena Kallick, I set out to design specific instructional strategies aimed at developing habits of mind. I read a variety of research in the areas of cognition and metacognition. I knew from experience that effective thinking has certain identifiable characteristics, and I was convinced that thoughtful classroom instruction could create the climate to teach those characteristics.

Teaching for thinking simply means that teachers strive to develop classroom conditions conducive to student thinking. Teachers pose problems and raise questions, and then follow up by introducing dilemmas, paradoxes, and discrepancies for students to resolve. Teachers also structure the classroom environment for thinking: They value thinking, make time for it, support it, and assess student growth in it. Teaching for thinking assumes a classroom atmosphere that balances trust, risk taking, and originality. I am confident this environment can be created anywhere because it is established through the behavior of a teacher who models respect for intelligence and establishes the clear, convincing expectation that all students can become better thinkers. In this kind of classroom you find an almost palpable sense of community that stems from collaboration and open investigation of ideas.

I planned to construct exercises that would provide a frame for analysis of literature, writing, self-evaluation, and observation. This construct was based on the knowledge that it is possible to connect teachable skills to a student's potential for responding to problems and ambiguities. I wanted to guide my students to recognize intelligent behavior, both academic and personal, as they approached the formation of argument for the expository essay. I also wanted them to recognize instances where literary characters reacted to conflict and resolved difficulties intelligently. I believed that if students could identify and articulate the ways in which characters used, or needed to use, more intelligent behavior, the students would begin to deepen their own understandings of the literary devices of character motivation, the author's choice of conflict, and thematic implications.

As we searched texts for clues about the connection between habits of mind and narrative development, I asked my students how they thought about their own work. What habits did they identify as essential to quality work? This was organic, really; it flowed naturally out of the literary analysis. Students came up with these habits: reading carefully, using dialectic notebooks to record intuitive responses, anticipating questions to clarify during class discussion, taking notes to record interpretation, and recognizing similarities to other works they'd read.

GATSBY AND THE HABITS OF MIND

When good thinkers study a text, they feel a sense of investigation, a deep curiosity, and an insistence on being accurate. Yet my one question remained: Although most of my students seemed to have the same ability to probe and discover the text, why didn't they? While we were studying *The Great Gatsby*, I asked students in my Advanced Senior Writing Seminar to analyze the novel in terms of the habits of mind. Beginning with basic discussions of the kinds of behavior apparent in the novel's main characters, they seemed to recognize quickly Jay Gatsby's creativity and persistence, Nick Carraway's wonderment and ability to listen to others, and Daisy Buchanan's impulsivity.

Moving beyond surface evaluations, I asked them to consider how the characters could have behaved more intelligently and to name alternative strategies the characters could have used. With their texts in one hand and the list of the habits of mind in the other, they explored the novel with little help from me. All their observations were formed first by their close reading of the text. But their understanding deepened when they pointed to specific instances where a systematic method of problem solving would have changed the direction of the novel's tragic outcome.

For example, they acknowledged that Nick Carraway had the advantages of being a careful listener and of drawing on past knowledge to change the course of his own life. This observation prompted them to think about themselves and their choices. In the course of this exploration, I saw a shift in the classroom from the teacher asking all the questions to students asking questions about the characters, which propelled further discussion. How did Nick make up his mind about Gatsby? What questions did Nick ask? How creative was Gatsby beyond his conception of himself?

Eventually, students drifted into conversations about their own habits of mind. Typically I would ask, "How, in fact, did you make up your mind about Nick? In what specific ways did you think about this novel? What were the literary devices that helped you to uncover character motivation, and, going further, to think about your own behavior, your own choices?"

In developing their essays about Nick, students were drawn to his steady voice in the midst of chaos. They decided his strength was his ability to approach conflict in alternate ways. Nick maintains his loyalty to Gatsby, even when all others have abandoned Gatsby, and he is mature in the face of the disorder around him. Nick is not a gossip or judge as he perseveres in his commitment to ensure that Gatsby's funeral be appropriate to his "romantic readiness." Students responded instinctively to Nick's allegiance to Gatsby when others just used his friend. Many of the students shared personal stories about times when they were compelled to stick by a friend when their own definition of loyalty was tested.

Sitting alone in my classroom at the end of June, I realized that I had waited too long to begin applying the habits of mind in our work. I was unsure about the short story as an entry point to the habits, and I lost about 10 weeks of what could have been very productive time. Obviously, the time was not totally wasted. I was helping students get accustomed to the vocabulary, breaking down the habits of mind, and working with selected habits. I know that the trust was there, and the playfulness of exercises like this appealed to students, especially because adolescent interest in learning more about the self is at its peak in 12th grade.

Though I regretted the lost time, I greatly valued the work we did. The essays analyzing *The Great Gatsby* were richer and more original because students had the power to criticize and suggest. The habits of mind became the touchstones for character analysis, and students gained a sense of power as they made resonant connections to their own behaviors. Students became enraged at Gatsby's naively romantic pursuit of Daisy, but they also defined what they knew about his flaws by using the habits as a frame. When they hypothesized about ideas, they arrived at much more pleasing and mature essays: "If Gatsby had been less impulsive, funneled his creativity into more than romance, recognized the strength of his creativity, then . . . ."

In the future, I'll begin work immediately in the fall by introducing the habits of mind and working them into all of our writing assignments, from the argumentative essay to the analysis of all literary genre. This time I will not hold back, because I know that I can rely on my curiosity and wonder to help students rediscover their own. Literature is the perfect conduit to understanding the self, a lesson I learn again and again with my students' help!

8

AN INTEGRATED APPROACH TO TEACHING THE HABITS OF MIND

NANCY SKERRITT AND EMILIE HARD

It has been estimated that 80 percent of the jobs available in the United States within 20 years will be cerebral and only 20 percent manual, the exact opposite of the ratio in 1900. A quadriplegic with good technical and communications skills is becoming a more valuable worker than an able-bodied person without those skills. . . . Minds will be preferred over muscle.

Jennifer James
Columnist for *The Seattle Times*

The Tahoma School District in Maple Valley, Washington, has worked aggressively to align its curriculum, instruction, and assessment with the skills students will need to live and work in the 21st century. To this end, the district adopted a profile that names six student outcomes: They will become collaborative workers, complex thinkers, quality producers, effective communicators, self-directed learners, and community contributors.

As the district created structures to support teachers' and students' work with these outcomes, it quickly became apparent that the outcomes contained an inherent need for directly teaching thinking processes and habits. For example, collaborative workers are flexible and show empathy. Complex thinkers demonstrate metacognition and problem-solving abilities. Quality producers are deliberate, not impulsive. Effective communicators demonstrate fluency and precision in language. Self-directed learners are persistent and inquisitive. Community contributors often take risks.

Eventually, the district adopted a thinking skills curriculum that identifies 20 thinking processes and 12 thinking habits, adapted from the work of Arthur L. Costa. In Tahoma's work with the habits of mind, the ultimate goal is for students to internalize and use the habits, not merely to recognize them in others.

THE CORE UNIT

Tahoma's curriculum has been written to intentionally incorporate direct instruction in thinking processes and habits. This work includes establishing unit outcomes and guiding questions, teaching introductory and application lessons, and then assessing students' application of thinking skills. The district has developed three core units at each grade level, K–6. (Work recently was completed on units at the secondary level.) These resources provide the structure for new and experienced teachers to help students acquire the characteristics described in the district's goals.

To show how Tahoma's curriculum weaves thinking habits throughout all classroom work, we highlight one of the core units: "Growth of a Nation." This unit is taught in 6th grade. Like all units, it begins with establishing an outcome and guiding questions, which provide focus and direction for both teacher and students. The following extract from the Tahoma School District Core Curriculum details this unit.

Growth of a Nation
Grade 6

Students will explore the Systems and Relationships that defined the growth of our nation during the Westward Movement and Civil War in order to develop the skills of Self-Directed Learners and Community Contributors in a democratic society.

1. What were the causes of the Westward Movement?
   - Storyboard Timeline
   - Trappers/Fur Traders
   - Homesteading
     - Oregon Trail
   - Religious Freedom
   - Manifest Destiny
     - Impact on Native Americans
   - Gold Rush/Wealth

- Outdoor Classroom Experiences

Teach **Cause and Effect** Thinking Skill

Teach **Persistence, Risk Taking**, and **Deliberativeness**
Thinking Behaviors

Apply **Finding Evidence** Thinking Skill

- Tall Tales
- Narrative Writing
  - Logs/Journals

2. What Systems and Relationships were evident before and during the
    Civil War?
    - Issues leading up to the war:
      - Economic Systems: Agrarian South vs. Industrial North
      - Social Systems: Human Rights-Slavery
      - Political Systems: Nation's vs. State's Rights
    - Relationships during the war:
      - Human Rights: Slavery/Underground Railroad
      - Major events of the war:
        - ❖ Famous battles and leaders
        - ❖ Gettysburg Address
        - ❖ Emancipation Proclamation

Apply **Point of View** and **Fact and Opinion** Thinking Skills

Apply **Empathy** Thinking Behavior

Reader's Workshop: Historical Fiction

Poetry Study: Langston Hughes

Civil War Reports and Presentations

3. How can we, as Americans living in a democracy, contribute to
    freedom and equality for all?
    - Martin Luther King Jr.
    - Human Rights issues today
    - Personal Goal-Setting: **Self-Directed Learner/Community
      Contributor** Service Projects
    - Multiple Intelligences Project Menu
    - Art Mural Project

The outcome statement clarifies a purpose for the unit. In this case,
students study the Westward Movement and Civil War to develop skills
related to being self-directed learners and community contributors. The
guiding questions help sequence the learnings and bring more specificity to
the unit outline, including which thinking processes and habits are taught
and applied.

Through the first guiding question, students explore the causes and effects of the westward movement. They apply the reading strategies of previewing, skimming, and summarizing as they find evidence for how early settlers demonstrated the habits of taking responsible risks, persisting, and managing implusivity. Teachers challenge learners to consider what these habits look and sound like. Naming these indicators enables students to understand the thinking behaviors in more concrete ways.

Students also use the indicators to search for evidence of the thinking habits. For example, students might say that Lewis and Clark were risk takers when they explored unfamiliar land and encountered dangerous animals. Early missionaries were persistent because they endured in the face of numerous obstacles. Homesteaders were deliberate as they carefully planned and prepared supplies for their journey.

Students can explore the content and thinking habits further through skits that depict settlers using a habit. For example, one skit might show that homesteaders sometimes had to travel with complete strangers, which illustrates risk taking. Another skit might show Brigham Young managing impulsivity by sending people ahead to create stopping places, build shelters, plant crops, and mark the trail.

Students notice that lack of a thinking habit sometimes contributes to an unsuccessful pursuit. Consider the gold prospector who perished because he wasn't deliberate enough to plan for adequate supplies during his trip to California. In another lesson, students compare and contrast traditional Native American values about the land and its resources with their own values. They begin to set goals for use of outdoor classroom sites, and they build on their experiences during the following lesson as they develop guidelines for exploring and enjoying nature (which also contributes to managing impulsivity). In the process, they examine their roles as community contributors.

Lessons intentionally provide for transfer of learnings to students' life experiences to make education more meaningful. As students reflect on times when they have been particularly persistent (perhaps when learning a sport or skill) or times when they were risk takers (meeting new friends, moving to a new area, trying new foods), they see how these habits of mind affect them personally. They connect thinking habits and goal achievement, and they come to understand why these habits are desirable.

As seen in the extract above, Guiding Questions 2 and 3 invite students to investigate the systems and relationships that were evident before, during, and after the Civil War. Empathy becomes the focus as students gain an in-depth understanding of northern and southern perspectives on slavery and human rights issues. Students examine the treatment of slaves, the

Underground Railroad, and the Emancipation Proclamation. They also investigate contemporary human rights issues by studying the poetry of Langston Hughes and the Civil Rights movement in the 1950s and '60s. The overall goal is for students to acquire the habit of empathy as they consider the perspectives of diverse people within a culture, overcome any racial hatred or bigotry, and develop genuine concern for the welfare of others.

EMPATHY IN ALL GRADES

As mentioned above, "Growth of a Nation" is taught in 6th grade. But we can trace the teaching of one of the habits it encompasses, empathy, throughout a student's career. For example, empathy is taught in 1st grade with a lesson on the picture book *The Rainbow Fish* by Marcus Pfister. The beautiful fish in the story learns kindness and helpful actions by sharing his scales with the other fish. After reading the story, students discuss the characteristics of empathy: helping others with kind actions and words, caring about other people, being concerned about problems that others face, asking questions to show concern, and looking at others when talking. The children use this understanding to create a "Code of Cooperation" for their classroom so that empathy becomes part of the culture of their learning environment.

At Grade 2 in the South America unit, students revisit the characteristics of empathy in relation to the story of "The Great Kapok Tree" by Lynne Cherry. Questions that guide the discussion include

1. How do you know the man became empathic in the story?
2. How and why did the man in the story develop empathy for the creatures of the rain forest?
3. How did having empathy affect his actions and behaviors?
4. Can you think of a time when you have felt empathy for an animal? Did this change your behavior or actions? How? Why?

In a 3rd grade unit on Africa, students explore folk tales. One of these is "Mufaro's Beautiful Daughters" by John Steptoe. Students evaluate which character in the story demonstrates the most empathy. Students also provide specific evidence for their choice.

A 4th grade unit on Asia has a lesson called "Cultural Contact." Students read *Encounter* by Jane Yolen to discuss cultural contact as depicted in the story. They examine the elements of the two cultures that are in conflict, and they identify the barriers that limit communication. Students explore how empathy is important when meeting people from different cultures. This concept is then transferred to exploring the diverse cultures of Asia. The children are challenged to consider their own experiences with cultural contact to expand point of view and develop sensitivity toward others.

In 5th grade, students conclude their study of the novel with *Number the Stars* by Louise Lowry. They are asked to find evidence of the Danish people's empathy toward others throughout the story. Students review the story elements of plot, character, setting, and theme as they list specific examples of empathy. Then students share how they can demonstrate empathy in their own lives, and they link empathy to the creation of a peaceful world. The children brainstorm ways to maintain peace among family members, school companions, or people in the community. They create a "Peace List" on a bulletin board and illustrate their ideas. Then they search for evidence of peacemaking acts in newspapers and magazines. As a class, they also create a "Peace Collage." This collage is a culmination of their study of the diverse cultures of Europe, and it reinforces the district goals of becoming effective communicators and collaborative workers.

WELL-GROUNDED STUDENTS

By the time students work with empathy in 6th grade, they are well-grounded in this thinking habit. As they begin "Growth of a Nation," they use dictionaries and thesauruses in an initial lesson to review empathy (see the template in Figure 8.1). They examine word parts to deepen understanding. They tell why it is important to have empathy for diverse perspectives, cultural differences, and varying challenges faced by people in the community. Then students create their own "Empathy Thinking Behavior Chart," using a template that prompts them to list what empathy looks like and sounds like (see Figure 8.2 on p. 110). These activities build on past experience, challenge students to think at deeper levels of understanding, and create ownership for the learning.

This establishing lesson is followed by application of empathy to human rights issues during the Civil War. Students read *Sweet Clara and the Freedom Quilt* by Deborah Hopkinson. They use three more thinking behaviors to investigate Sweet Clara's character in the story: originality, persistence, and inquisitiveness. Students next discuss examples of empathy in

FIGURE 8.1
Defining *Empathy*

Recall what the word *empathy* means.
Use a dictionary to look up and record the definition of the word *empathy*. Include the origin of the word.
Use a thesaurus to look up synonyms for the word *empathy*.
Tell why it is important to have *empathy* for the diverse perspectives, cultural differences, and different challenges faced by people in our community.

Source: Excerpted from Tahoma School District Core Curriculum, Maple Valley, Washington.

the story. Students work in groups of four to create a collage that demonstrates empathy. They use magazine pictures; illustrations; and their own graphics, slogans, or labels to represent the concept of empathy. Finally, they use an empathy performance checklist to self-assess their progress in demonstrating empathetic behaviors (see Figure 8.3 on p. 111).

Students also weave empathy into selections about historical events from *War, Terrible War* by Joy Hakim. For example, students read about Lee's surrender to Grant and consider how each leader demonstrates empathy toward the other at this climactic event of the Civil War. Students are encouraged to model empathy as they role-play this scene. Finally, students reflect on what it means to live in a democracy by writing about the core beliefs "all men are created equal" and all are entitled to "life, liberty, and the pursuit of happiness."

Many other habits of mind are woven into Guiding Questions 2 and 3. Students apply risk taking to an exploration of the Underground Railroad. They brainstorm characteristics of risk takers, apply these

FIGURE 8.2
Empathy Thinking Behavior Chart

List the behaviors that would demonstrate what *empathy* looks like.
List the behaviors that would demonstrate what *empathy* sounds like.

Source: Excerpted from Tahoma School District Core Curriculum, Maple Valley, Washington.

characteristics to Harriet Tubman, discuss how many people were risk takers in helping slaves to freedom, and reflect on risks they have taken in their own lives. Attending and persistence are applied to work students do in exploring major battles of the Civil War. Students practice the skill of skimming for information, complete a "Battle Matrix" with facts about major battles, and then self-evaluate their efforts with a performance checklist that incorporates expectations for demonstrating the two targeted habits of mind.

Guiding Question 2 culminates with a project entitled "The Civil War Hall of Fame." Students select one famous leader from a list that includes Abraham Lincoln, Robert E. Lee, Ulysses S. Grant, Harriet Beecher Stowe, Harriet Tubman, and Sojourner Truth. Students take notes, produce a written report, create a visual presentation, and give an oral presentation. An important component of the project is to identify three habits of mind that the Civil War leader demonstrates. This evidence provides the basis for nominating the person to the Civil War Hall of Fame.

The evaluation criteria for all aspects of the project are completely centered on the habits of mind. The students and the teacher evaluate each component of the assignment according to criteria connected to a specific habit. Note taking is linked to managing impulsivity and being inquisitive; the written report is judged for fluency, elaboration, and persistence; the visual presentation is connected to standards for originality and precision; and the oral presentation is linked to risk taking. Students use the habits of mind to assess their own performance, internalizing standards for personal achievement.

FIGURE 8.3

A Checklist to Self-Assess Progress

Name: _____ Date: _____

Showing Sensitivity and Understanding Toward Others

EMPATHY PERFORMANCE CHECKLIST		
Indicators: I demonstrate these behaviors . . .	**Yes**	**No**
Helpful Actions • Acts of Kindness		
Attentive Listening • Paraphrasing • Spending time talking		
Concerned Expressions • Head nodding in agreement • Similar emotions		
Interested Questions • "Tell me more." • "I want to understand."		
Affirming Statements • "I understand." • "I care about you." • "I want to help you."		

Source: Excerpted from Tahoma School District Core Curriculum, Maple Valley, Washington.

Figure 8.4 (see p. 112) shows the scoring rubric used to evaluate the Civil War Hall of Fame project. The total score in each category is weighted so that the total possible points for the project equal 100. Teachers can then easily convert the project grade to a letter grade.

Habits of mind are equally important in other subject areas. For example, efforts to integrate math content with core units has resulted in applications such as "Glenda Gold-digger." Students are presented with a gold prospector who needs to determine the amount and worth of the grams of gold in her collection. Teachers reinforce persistence as students use different approaches to the problem. Students use the habit of metacognition as

FIGURE 8.4
Civil War Hall of Fame Scoring Rubric

Name: _____   Date: _____

Scoring Scale

4 = Exemplary   3 = Consistently   2 = Sometimes   1 = Rarely   NS = Not Scorable

NOTE-TAKING

Managing Impulsivity
Score: _____
• Intentionally sought and gathered essential information
• Used a variety of sources
• Accurately interpreted information

Inquisitiveness
Score: _____
• Displayed an enthusiasm for exploration and sought new learning
• Looked for additional information
• Made connections with past learning

Total score: _____ X 2 = _____

ORAL PRESENTATION

Risk Taking
Score: _____
• Demonstrated the ability to perform in front of a group by speaking and clearly using good eye contact
• Showed evidence of being comfortable by expressing information in an original way

Total score: _____ X 3 = _____

WRITTEN REPORT

Fluency
Score: _____
• Often showed evidence of a variety of ideas
• Clearly supported main ideas with sufficient information
• Showed evidence that ideas and concepts flowed together easily

Elaboration
Score: _____
• Demonstrated the use of multiple resources to develop own thinking
• Showed evidence of higher-level thinking process: analysis, synthesis, evaluation, and application
• Clarified thinking and added details

Persistence
Score: _____
• Effectively made attempts to communicate clearly by focusing on relevant information and clear organization
• Persevered at using correct mechanics
• Usually displayed an understanding of the importance of readability by having a legible report

Total score: _____ X 4 = _____

VISUAL PRESENTATION

Originality
Score: _____
• Created a unique product that showed evidence of taking risks and using unique approaches
• Showed interesting information about the subject

Precision
Score: _____
• Showed evidence of comparing work to criteria and checking for accuracy
• Displayed evidence of careful use of tools and materials

Total score: _____ X 3 = _____

Total Points for Project _____ (100 points possible)

Source: Excerpted from Tahoma School District Core Curriculum, Maple Valley, Washington.

112

they explain the steps in their strategies and reflect on the effectiveness of those strategies and the reasonableness of their solutions.

The habits of mind are woven extensively throughout all of Tahoma's units. The district strives to structure the acquisition of content through the lens of thinking strategies and habits as identified in the thinking skills curriculum. We use these habits and skills to enhance content learning, to promote connections to life experience, and to encourage self-reflection. Assessing the habits of mind is ongoing and embedded throughout the various lessons as illustrated in several of the examples we have provided. In addition, we have developed instruction and assessment tools based on Costa's notion that we must consider what it looks like and sounds like to demonstrate these habits.

As in many U.S. schools, Tahoma's students are accountable to state standards and are assessed on tests that require far more than the traditional recall of information. We are pleased that our schools have shown continued improvement in reading, writing, and mathematics as measured on these and other examinations. We believe that the emphasis we have placed on teaching thinking skills and habits is at the heart of our students' success. As Costa says, the true measure of success is not in knowing the right answer, but in knowing what to do when you don't know the answer. It is our belief that developing habits of mind will best equip our students for living and working in the 21st century.

9

DISCOVERING HABITS OF MIND IN MATHEMATICS

CAROL T. LLOYD

Perhaps this story is familiar to you. I teach in North Carolina where the state mandates curriculum for every subject and every grade, which teachers are required by law to follow. The state also mandates an end-of-grade testing program for grades 3–8 and end-of-course testing for grades 9–12. These tests, of course, are based on the prescribed curriculum. School systems, individual schools, and, to some extent, even individual teachers are evaluated on students' scores on these tests. Obviously, this structure leaves little freedom for individual schools or teachers to spend much time outside the mandated curriculum.

The good news, however, is that this lack of freedom is pushing needed curriculum changes. Over the last ten years, the state has implemented two new math curriculums for grades K–12, which also has changed the corresponding testing program. These changes include testing students on their abilities to use the calculator as a tool for solving problems, to communicate mathematical ideas with words and drawings, and to solve various types of problem situations. To gain time for teaching such operations and processes, we have deemphasized mastery of basic skills that can be done by calculators. It's more important for students to be able to take a problem situation, organize it for input into the calculator, and use the resulting answers or graphs for data analysis and prediction. As we move toward more of this kind of mathematical thinking, it's obvious that classrooms must nourish the development of habits of mind.

Source: Costa, A., & Liebmann, R. (Eds.), *Envisioning Process as Content: Toward a Renaissance Curriculum*, pp. 95–106, copyright © 1997 by Sage Publications, Inc. Adapted by permission of the author and Sage Publications, Inc.

SUPPORTING THE HABITS OF MIND

For the last nine years, I have worked on developing the habits of mind with my students. I know I must support students by pointing out examples of where habits of mind have been used, showing where they could have been used, and providing opportunities for students to display the habits. I also know that I constantly must model these behaviors. Students should see their teacher experience failure. They should see their teacher model persistence, metacognition, a sense of humor, and then flexibility by applying a number of problem-solving strategies until finding one that works. Through these performances, students see how I achieve a greater level of problem-solving efficacy, and they see how they can attain the same successes, too.

Students who do not feel efficacious about their ability to succeed often are unwilling to tackle problem situations. Yet students must accept responsibility for their own learning. They need opportunities to figure things out on their own or with the help of other students. I must not jump in too quickly to answer their questions or solve their problems. Assignments should be completed for the contribution they make to the student's learning process, not just to satisfy me.

I have observed students' sense of efficacy grow as they experience success in an environment that scaffolds their learning, encourages failing forward, and keeps the risk-taker safe from humiliation. One student, Mia, came to me as a sophomore quite sure that math was not her subject. She was an excellent student in all classes, but she felt math was her weakness. She saw it as something to be tolerated because she had no choice. Her attitude changed a great deal because of her experiences in my class. In fact, by the time she reached advanced math her junior year, she had become the one the other students turned to for help—and she knew she could help them.

Students become interdependent by working in an environment that requires them to be interdependent and rewards them for being so. The classroom environment should support the idea of "a journey we are taking together," not "teacher versus students" or "student versus student." The teacher should not be viewed as the person with all the answers. Groups of students (and their teachers) should be viewed as a learning community. Once again, the teacher's modeling is extremely important. The teacher must model the idea that we are all smarter together than we are alone. Students should see teachers working together with other teachers and with students to plan and solve all types of activities and problems. Students should also be asked for their input. For example, students can easily provide the teacher with feedback about classroom procedures and activities. Cooperative learning techniques also give students practice with interdependent behaviors they will be required to use outside the classroom.

Activities that develop students' problem-solving abilities support the habits of mind of metacognition, flexibility, and precision. The two questions I most often ask students are "How did you get that?" and "Why did you do it that way?" Just getting the answer is not what is most important. The next time the answer will be different. What matters is the student's understanding of the process used to arrive at the answer so that it can be refined, altered, or repeated for later problems. "I got that answer, but I'm not sure how," is not acceptable. In an atmosphere of constant questioning, students are forced to clarify their thought processes, analyze their errors, and refine their own questions.

By supporting and appreciating diversity of methods, we teach flexibility. Students who are required to do things in exactly one way will have difficulty dealing with ambiguity, finding alternative ways to solve any type of problem, or trying something when they are not sure what to do.

Math teachers are notorious for inflexibility because of their own learning styles and their belief that mathematics is an "exact" science. Yet we must be willing to model flexibility in many ways. In my classroom, flexibility has been one of the hardest things for some students to accept. For so long, students have been told to follow certain directions and to do it "just this way." They are often at a loss when I refuse to provide specific parameters. Certainly, some things are mathematically incorrect, but mathematics also encompasses much more flexibility and ambiguity than most of my students have been led to believe. If they are to survive in a constantly changing society, then they must appreciate and practice flexibility.

Appreciating flexibility does not preclude striving for excellence and producing high-quality work. In the fast-food, throw-away society of the United States, students often don't gain an understanding of what constitutes high quality. Whatever we ask students to produce—a homework assignment, an essay question, a project—we continually must work to develop their appreciation for and understanding of what a high-quality product is. When we see positive changes in the quality of their work, their writing, their questioning, and their responses, then we know they are striving for higher levels of precision and accuracy.

PROCESSING EXPERIENCES

Keeping a journal is often suggested as a way of supporting growth in students' thinking skills. Many times my students are surprised by the "writing" they have to do for math class, writing that begins on the first day! Yet as time goes on, this journal time provides an opportunity for students to be creative, thoughtful, and reflective. Some children find this time the most rewarding part of my class.

The fact that they are given a grade based on their thoughtful completion of assignments each quarter reinforces the importance I place on their thinking and writing. At first they don't believe I actually will read their journals. When I return journals with supportive comments and specific feedback, students realize I am serious about their writing. When I make comments in class about the feedback and suggestions they give me—and then act accordingly—their ownership of the class increases, as does their belief that they can make a difference.

Early in the year, I must be open and willing to accept whatever responses I get. This approach also requires great flexibility on my part. I remember one student in Algebra II who started the year quite sure that he would never pass my class. He had barely passed Algebra I. During the second week in school, I asked him to explain why a negative number times a negative number is a positive. He had not a clue. He did, however, respond quite creatively with a poem, which ended, "Why ask why, ask why?" When he volunteered to read his response the next day, I applauded his sense of humor and his creativity. He soon began to display other intelligent behaviors, such as persistence and questioning. I am happy to report he passed my class and went on to a four-year college, intent on a degree in nursing.

Here are some examples of the types of questions I have given for journal assignments. They are not specifically math questions, but they support the processing of students' learning and provide me feedback about our class:

- "When I hear the word math I think _____ and I feel _____."
- "Problem solving means _____."
- "The hardest thing about problem solving is _____."
- "I took this course because _____."

• Ask students to analyze a class activity: "What did you like and what did you not like about the activity? What did it help to clarify for you? What is still not clear?"

• After the first few cooperative learning activities, ask students what they did and did not like about them. For example, how did the group follow directions, work together, and communicate?

• To practice metacognition, ask students to explain some task or problem and how they thought it through.

• Ask students to think of a nonmath problem they've had in the last few months. Ask them to describe how they solved the problem and at least two other ways they could have solved it.

• Have students compare and contrast concepts learned. For example, after learning four methods for solving a system of linear equations, I might ask students to compare and contrast using the four methods. Which one seems the easiest or most efficient to them more often? Why do they seem to prefer one over the others?

• Ask students to propose criteria and their rationale for evaluation of a project. Follow this work with a class discussion in which they must reach a decision on the criteria for grading.

• Ask students to describe which two habits of mind they display most often. Which two have they improved most? How and when do they display them? Which two do they have the most trouble using? How can they improve in these areas? Which two habits of mind do you, the teacher, most need to improve? Ask for suggestions of how you might work on those areas.

• As a review assignment, have students explain what concepts they should understand as result of a unit. What should they be expected to know for a test? Have them make possible questions for a test.

• After they complete a project, ask students to evaluate it. What skills or concepts did they have to use? What did they learn from completing the project? What habits of mind did they have to use? How did they use them?

• When you try new things in the classroom, have your students give you feedback. Was the new strategy helpful to them? Why or why not? What suggestions do they have for making it better the next time?

• Ask students to use a Venn diagram for comparing and contrasting characteristics of themselves with two other family members.

• Before or after holidays or other big events (like the prom), have students describe using habits of mind in that special situation.

• Have students analyze a test situation. Was the test what they expected? How did they prepare for the test? What should they do again or do differently next time?

• Ask students to create new habits of mind they feel should be practiced. Ask them to explain these habits.

Students' journals have provided me with some of the most accurate assessments of my teaching and student learning. Sometimes students are painfully honest, especially after they know I will not hold their comments against them. Sometimes I agree with their assessments; other times I don't. For example, several years ago, my honors students, who are mostly sophomores, had difficulty accepting some of my teaching practices. Because I did not tell them they had to do certain problems a certain way, they were confused by the ambiguity. Because I did not check their homework every day, they did not always do their assignments. As a result, many of them were not pleased by the grades they received. I even had a guidance counselor work with them one day so they could air their complaints.

When students realized I was not going to give in and accept responsibility for their lack of responsibility, they began to work harder. At the end of first semester, I asked them to consider what they needed to do differently second semester. I also asked them what the teacher and their parents could do to support them. Almost without exception, they said that we needed to encourage them, but they agreed that the responsibility for the learning was theirs.

Another way I have provided processing experiences for my students is through projects. I pose the following problem: "For your birthday I am going to give you a present: a big dog. In order for you to be ready, I am going to give you the material for a doghouse ahead of time. I'll give you one piece of plywood, four feet by eight feet, and some nails. You have a saw, a ruler, and a hammer. Your goal is to design and build (on paper) the biggest doghouse you can." We talk about the fact that they will need to define for themselves what constitutes a doghouse and how they will determine "the biggest."

On the day they bring in their projects, we have a class discussion to establish a definition for "doghouse" and how we will determine "the biggest." These discussions can become very heated! By the time we have finished our discussions and tried to determine the biggest, students are amazed by how much math and how many habits of mind they have used. Often, students comment in their reflective journals that next time they will think much longer when confronted by what seems to be an easy, little assignment!

Thoughtful Decision Making

I am constantly appalled to find my students lack the knowledge of how to make a thoughtful decision. The problem, I suppose, is that the responsibility to teach decision-making skills does not fall under any specific curriculum. Many of my students are not taught those skills by their families either. Several years ago, I decided I would not let my juniors and seniors graduate from high school without at least one formal experience in decision making.

Students may choose their own decision to make. Most work on choices for college or careers, but I also have had students decide when would be the best time to get married or what to buy someone for a present. Figure 9.1 shows the project as it is presented to students. The way in which they are to document later steps is discussed with them in class as we go through the project. Many students have told me through the years that this project was the most important thing they learned in my class.

Assessment

Assessment is another area in which I have experimented with my students. I have attempted to use a variety of formal test questions, including the type of open-ended questions that now are showing up in testing programs. The world outside school does not always function through multiple-choice or fill-in-the-blank tasks or evaluations. Students must experience, in the relative safety of the classroom, the unstructured, ill-defined problems they will encounter in life.

As I began to make so many changes in my teaching practices, I felt the need for some "hard" data about my progress. My end-of-course test scores have remained fairly stable, usually with a slight increase from year to year. Yet these were not the data for which I searched. Much of what I was doing was not assessed by state tests. Finally, I developed a student survey that I administered two years in a row. Students answered anonymously.

Although the hard data from the survey were encouraging, "soft" data like the following story warm my heart. Several years ago, one of my students, Rita, was in a minor car accident on the way to school. As she sat in the office waiting for her parents to arrive, the assistant principal tried to keep Rita's mind occupied by asking her about her classes and teachers. When Rita told her she was in my class, the principal asked how she felt about that. Her response was, "She makes you think so hard your head hurts!"

FIGURE 9.1
Decision-Making Project

The Steps in the Process:

1. Define the problem. What decision do I have to make?
2. Identify areas of concern. What are my options? (This step often requires research.)
3. Predict consequences. List for each option the positive and negative possible outcomes. (This step usually requires research.)
4. Prioritize. What is the likelihood of that consequence occurring and how important is it to my decision?
5. Assess sources. How reliable is each source from which I received information? Is the information objective?
6. Make a decision. Based upon the information gathered, what is the best choice for you?

We will discuss each of the steps in the process during class. You will individually keep a record of the process for your own decision. At the end of the project, you will be expected to turn in a clear, well-organized presentation of the process you have completed. You will be graded on the evidence of the thoroughness of your process and the clarity of your presentation. Each step not completed and checked on time will result in a loss of 3 points per day late. The project will count as one test grade.

Step	*Due Date*
1. Decision to be made	November 17
2. List of options	November 21 and 29
3. Possible outcomes	December 1
4. Prioritize outcomes	December 6
5. Assessment of sources	December 6
6. Make a decision	December 9

Name: _____

Step 1. What decision do I have to make?

_____

_____

I have watched my own children go off to school filled with wonder and a joy of learning that I rarely see in my students. My vision, shared by many others, is to develop schools that nourish and support rather than stifle that wonder and joy. I often remind my Algebra II students about the limitations of their math knowledge. Just as a 1st grader may say you can't subtract 3 from 1, or a 3rd grader may say you can't divide 2 by 5, my students will tell me you can't divide by zero. My response is that's true with real numbers, but you'll come close in calculus. When they say there is no square root of -4, I agree that there is no real answer to the square root of a negative number; they will have to wait until second semester when we expand the world of real numbers to the complex numbers, which include imaginary numbers.

I want students to continually wonder about what still lies ahead on their learning journey. This idea was expressed best in a statement made by my minister: "As your island of knowledge grows, so grows your shoreline of wonder." Nurturing both knowledge and wonder is my role as a teacher; I happen to use mathematics as the vehicle to reach that goal.

10

AN ARTISTIC APPLICATION OF HABITS OF MIND

NADINE McDERMOTT

A firm grounding in the arts teaches practical skills and such characteristics as self-discipline and critical thinking. The arts naturally embrace paradox and ambiguity; to study them is to learn flexible thinking. Those who have trained in an art form are more likely not only to grasp the nuances in real life, say the experts, but also to persevere in finding novel solutions to everyday problems.

Susan Gaines, "The Art of Living"

The stage was set at the Bronxville School in Bronxville, New York: no windows, 52 black chairs, a Steinway grand piano, a portable chalkboard, students, and teacher. The students arrived to participate in a music class requiring multidimensional processes that were physical, intellectual, and emotional. The teacher's goals were clear to her: Teach these students to sing, and prepare them for a musical performance twice a year. The students' goals also seemed clear: to enjoy 48 minutes socializing with their friends and spend very little time singing.

In typical adolescent fashion, cliques started to surface. More socializing than singing occurred, and the teacher began to feel more like a referee than an educator. The teacher tried every trick in the educational bag to create a serious, educational learning environment, with limited success.

This vignette captures the essence of a classroom situation that was very real. Aware that this situation could not continue, I reviewed the curriculum, and, with other department members, I decided to investigate alternative approaches to music education, including assessment. With the National Standards for Arts Education (1994) in one hand and the latest research on multiple intelligences (Gardner, 1983) in the other, we knew we had to decide how we could incorporate these essentially new ideas into our work with students. We also decided that we needed to take another look at the traditional method of using biannual performances as "assessment."

NECESSARY CHANGE

In 1991, department members visited the Pittsburgh Public Schools to observe the Harvard Project Zero Arts PROPEL Pilot Project in action. The educational benefits of this program were obvious and valid. That visit forever changed my perspective of music education and, ultimately, my teaching.

After we returned from Pittsburgh, we agreed as a department to recreate a curriculum that would include alternative forms of assessment contained in a portfolio. After piloting one project from Arts PROPEL, we understood that this new approach required behavioral changes for both the teacher and the students. In monitoring students' growth over time, I discovered that although they were becoming skilled music critics, their behavior didn't change.

Individual and class detentions, telephone calls to parents, and discussions with the administration and my department chair did not remedy the situation. Students continued to act out. Students who came to socialize still held a daily "tea party." Students who truly were interested in learning had difficulty staying interested and retaining skills and concepts because of distractions created by the other students.

WHAT TO DO?

The traditional behavioral management plan obviously was not effective. I had to shift my style from punishing students to convincing students to change their behavior in positive directions. The challenge was to find information on this topic so the situation could be remedied.

In the course of my search, a colleague shared with me a handout on the habits of mind (at that time called "intelligent behaviors"), which he had received at a workshop. After discussing this handout with members of my department, we made a conscious decision to include the habits of mind and Gardner's multiple intelligences as part of the middle and high school music curriculum. The habits of mind would be an integral part of the intrapersonal skill development in each music class, skills that would be taught *and* assessed.

Implementing the habits of mind into the traditional 8th grade choral rehearsal was the next hurdle. I was eager to try this new concept, but I struggled with giving up rehearsal time for class discussion on a "nonmusical" topic. What would the benefits be? Would it be possible to change students' behavior this way? I finally summoned enough courage to try.

I began by having the class define the word "habits." I then passed out a list of the habits of mind. We read the habits aloud and considered how behaviors gradually form habits. After a lengthy discussion, which ranged from defining unfamiliar words to how these habits of mind could be applied to chorus, I gave students an assignment. They were asked to write a paragraph about each habit, describing how each applied to chorus. As this experiment grew in size and depth, a colleague discovered Theodore Sizer's "intellectual habits" (Sizer, 1992), which we added to our repertoire.

In developing and implementing the nonmusical part of the curriculum, I could see that we were providing tools for students to function more effectively in a large group. I began to think of ways this new concept could be incorporated into rehearsals with purpose and meaning. Ways to assess student progress in this new area soon followed.

I created an assignment that asked the students to describe the similarities and differences between Costa's habits of mind and Sizer's intellectual habits. In addition, students had to choose two habits and describe how each was illustrated by work in their portfolio. The conclusion of this assignment required students to reflect on their interactions with others in chorus. They had to describe one specific example of a behavior or attitude that reflected their growth in developing the skills needed for interdependence in an ensemble.

I saw noticeable improvement in students' behavior, which ultimately resulted in improved student performance. Consciously and subconsciously, I modeled the habits of mind with and for the students. During rehearsal, I frequently announced when certain habits of mind were being modeled. In working with the tenor and bass section in the 8th grade chorus, for example, it was essential that the soprano and alto sections display empathy. The changing adolescent voice is difficult to train. Boys at this age frequently stop singing because they don't know how to use the instrument any more and because they don't want to be ridiculed by their peers if their voices crack.

Validation

The biannual school concerts proved the benefit of intentionally incorporating the habits of mind into rehearsal. The chorus's performance reflected a greater degree of musical precision and accuracy, and the chorus gained respect from the audience and the other ensembles in the department. The phrase "I don't know" no longer was permitted in class. Students now had strategies to use when an answer was not obvious to them. Students could express uncertainty by saying, "I'm not quite sure, but I think the answer might be . . . ," or "Could you please restate the question?" I encouraged students to use the habits of mind in searching for the solution to a question. This concept provoked students to learn how to learn and thus encouraged independent learning in a large-group setting. The ensemble now functioned more effectively.

As time went on, the habits of mind became a strong thread woven into the fabric of every rehearsal. The habits helped increase student awareness of their behavior so they could monitor themselves, which affected the ensemble positively. We videotaped a portion of a selected piece. While students watched and listened to the videotape, they completed an Arts PROPEL Ensemble Critique from the *Arts PROPEL Handbook for Music* (Davidson et al., n.d.). This assessment required students to diagnose and prescribe solutions to musical problems. A specific response was essential for a student to score at the advanced level. Coaching students to use all the habits of mind during this assessment ultimately improved their performance. My role went from choral "director" to "instructional guide." I created the environment in which independent, self-directed learning occurred in an interdependent, ensemble setting.

Another Opportunity

The true test came when I took a vocal music position in another school district. When students arrived on the first day, I thought I had everything prepared. The students received a handout, clearly outlining the course goals and requirements. After numerous attempts to get their attention, I began doubting what I had learned in my previous position. With a great deal of persistence and flexible thinking, I accomplished the day's plan and admonished those who needed to return with better rehearsal "habits."

This new situation paralleled my previous position in that students were not used to singing in chorus and certainly did not view rehearsal as an academic class. After assessing the class, I identified several weak areas. The students were musically illiterate and vocally untrained. Their perceptions about chorus were casual at best. All the evidence pointed toward a need for exposure to the habits of mind. Weighing all the factors, I decided to introduce the habits of mind to the accelerated chorus first. These students had auditioned the previous year and were selected to be members of this ensemble. These 23 students were in the class because of their commitment and willingness to accept the challenge of taking a high school course in middle school. I quickly discovered that was not the case entirely! They, too, were not taking chorus to become skilled, trained musicians.

To introduce the habits of mind, I followed the same lesson plan that I used in my previous district, but I added a reflective journal component. I left time at the end of rehearsal for students to reflect on what habits of mind they had used and how they used them. We shared the reflections at the beginning of the next rehearsal. Rehearsals were more productive, and all but a few students began to realize the positive changes. To ensure that these habits of mind remained an integral part of every rehearsal, I developed a daily plan, a type of itinerary that delineated our musical objectives and asked a guiding question about what habits of mind would be used to reach our musical destination. I first shared this approach with students using a song for which we had very little time to prepare for the performance. The students had to maintain a daily journal. In the sample student journal entries below, I have added in brackets the habits of mind the students were describing. Here are the entries:

- "I think that I have a better understanding of what we have to accomplish and in what amount of time. I hope this is another interesting way to learn music that I can carry with me to learn other pieces of music [drawing on past knowledge]. I think by limiting us to four days, we all focused on doing things right the first time [accuracy and precision]."
- "I feel that if the Select Choir continues to behave like this during class, our spring concert will be extremely rewarding. I also learned that I can retain music faster [efficacy]. I feel that the journal entries force us to reevaluate what we did in class and focus on the areas that we need help with [metacognition]. By doing this and becoming aware of our mistakes, we are forcing ourselves to pay particularly close attention to these areas and correcting our mistakes [accuracy and precision, metacognition, persistence]. It only took me 5 periods, 210 minutes, less than 4 hours to learn this piece of music. I am excited with my progress as a musician."

These student examples reflect the initial stage of this new way of thinking and behaving. The impact was obvious, and I was compelled by students' rapid progress. For these reasons, I incorporated the habits of mind in every lesson and in every assessment. As a result, a common language developed among the ensemble members. They also developed a mutual understanding of how musicians were to behave in rehearsal. A student wrote, "I believe that some of the simplest of skills that I learned in that room will guide me through some of the most difficult parts of my life in the future." Another student wrote, "I don't know is not an acceptable answer. In class, you must try to answer the question by drawing on past knowledge." Another wrote, "I am glad we learned these [habits of mind] because I became more conscientious about the way that I acted in school. I learned how to become a better student." This validation was incentive enough for me to refine the implementation of habits of mind in rehearsal.

THE SECOND YEAR

Knowing that I was getting a new group of students who were not familiar with the habits of mind, I realized I had to introduce the habits within the first month. In doing so, I saw a very responsive group of students ready to meet the challenges that were ahead. One student proclaimed, "Habits of mind are used every day to help me reach my goals. In order to overcome my weaknesses, metacognition is very important. Using habits of mind doesn't necessarily mean you know all of the answers, but it means you know what to do when you don't know the answer." Another student remarked, "The habits of mind helped me a great deal to organize my thinking. I have used flexibility in thinking to help me realize that there is not always one way of doing something. It has taught me to think about the different solutions to a problem before rushing ahead with the first solution I come up with."

The level of productivity in rehearsal increased tremendously. Students more consistently demonstrated the behaviors of musicians. When I used the phrase, "demonstrate the habits of mind of a musician" in rehearsal, the response was immediate: Students sat with correct posture, and they held their music accurately, pencil in hand, prepared for their first entrance.

MUSICIANS' HABITS OF MIND

Training students to become skilled musicians is a complex task, both cognitive and physical in nature. Decoding the music symbol system requires the same process of sound-symbol correspondence as reading. (For example, this is what the word looks like and this is what it sounds like. In music, this is what the musical phrase looks like and this is what it sounds like.) A musician literally must "think in sound." While the cognitive processes of thinking in sound are taking place, the musician is also producing the sound either by playing an instrument, which is an extension of the body, or by using the voice, which is an intangible instrument. A musician must condition the mind, which conditions the body to physically produce the sound, while at the same time cognitively decoding the notation in the musical score to create musical meaning. These complex functions of mind and body require the musician to use metacognition to experience growth and progress.

The habits of mind create an avenue for students to organize their thinking as musicians. Throughout students' training, I intentionally identify the attributes of musicians both from a cognitive and physical aspect. The following journal entries reflect how students used the habits to organize their thinking:

- "During the winter concert, we learned how to assign solfège syllables to the notes. In preparation for the spring concert, we drew on past knowledge and assigned solfège syllables to the notes in our new songs."
- "Curiosity led us down another path of exploration. If there was an unfamiliar symbol somewhere in the music, we identified the symbol and its purpose."
- "I believe one of the habits of mind that has helped us the most was decreasing impulsivity. Since the beginning of the year, we have all become so much more independent, yet we can still work well together as an ensemble. Before, if we had a question, our hands would shoot up and a lot of teacher calling and 'ooohhhhing' would go on. Now, when we have a question, we think about it and listen to others. Only if it is extremely important and pertains to the lesson do we finally ask the question. We no longer have to waste time on inappropriate questions and pointless babble."

- "Almost each and every day, our choir used persistence while learning this piece. It takes a great deal of effort to continuously work hard and not get frustrated. Our choir, though we did not sing everything correctly at first glance, persevered until we got it right."

- "I have used flexibility in thinking to help me realize that there is not always one way of doing something. It has taught me to think about the different solutions to a problem before rushing ahead with the first solution I come up with."

- "Checking for accuracy and precision was another intelligent behavior used in learning this piece. The choir continued to work and strive for the goal to make 'America The Beautiful' as accurate and precise as we could and we would not settle for anything less."

When habits of mind are embedded in the learning process of becoming a musician, the end product for students is empowerment to learn. Metacognition allows students to self-reflect, assess, and direct their own learning. Their experience is rich with strategies and multiple solutions. The study of music promotes inductive as well as deductive reasoning because many musical problems have more than one correct solution.

The National Standards for Arts Education clearly outline what students should know and be able to do. The skills, concepts, and knowledge to meet those standards cannot be obtained in a traditional rehearsal setting. Only through the habits of mind (and alternative forms of assessment) are my students able to meet those standards and, even more, become highly skilled, intelligent musicians.

REFERENCES

Davidson, L., Myford, C., Plasket, D., Scripp, L., Swinton, S., Torff, B., and Waanders, J. (n.d.). *Arts PROPEL Handbook for Music*. Pittsburgh, PA: Pittsburgh Public School System.

Gardner, H. (1983). *Frames of mind*. New York: BasicBooks.

National standards for arts education: What every young American should know and be able to do in the arts. (1994). Reston, VA: Music Educators National Conference.

Sizer, T. (1992). *Horace's school: Redesigning the American high school*. New York: Houghton Mifflin.

11

FOREIGN LANGUAGE INSTRUCTION AND THE "SENSE-SATIONAL" HABITS OF MIND

GINA CELESTE COSTA

Consider the following three stories, which originally were presented to students in a foreign language class learning Spanish:

Juan's class wants to have a party. Juan offers to go to the store. He drives his Ferrari to the local Safeway. He is in a great hurry. Juan grabs some chips and soda and throws them into the cart. Then he rushes to the deli section and tosses some mild red chili salsa into the cart. He runs to the checkout counter and pays $20 for the snacks and drives back to school. The students look at the food and say, "Yum!" Juan opens the mild red chili salsa. The students dip in their chips and put them in their mouths. "AYYYYYY!!!" they shout. The salsa is mislabeled!! It is really EXTRA, EXTRA HOT!!! The teacher calls the fire department!!! The firefighters spray water all over the students. The principal gets mad at the teacher and the class goes home.

Katerina is very, very tired. She decides to go to bed. She brushes her teeth, washes her face, and puts on her pajamas. She checks the doors, picks up the cat, and turns off all the lights. She hops into bed, caresses the cat, and closes her eyes for the night. Suddenly, she sits bolt upright in her bed! There is a very loud sound coming from the house next door!!! She realizes that it is the sound of snoring!! She jumps out of bed, throws open the window, and shouts at the man to stop snoring!! The man stops for a while. Soon the sound of snoring is too loud for Katerina to bear!!!

She calls the police, and they arrest Katerina's neighbor and haul him off to jail. Finally Katerina goes to sleep peacefully and doesn't wake up until noon the next day.

Valerie is in Paris. She will be there for three days and nights. She is so excited because it is her first trip to the City of Lights. She plans to visit many places, but what she really wants to do is see the lights of the city from the top of the Eiffel Tower. The first night Valerie tries to get a taxi to the tower, but none is available. The second night she takes the subway to the tower, but the elevator workers there are on strike and she cannot go up. The third night Valerie is very worried. She really wants to see the city all lit up!!! Once again she arrives at the tower. The line is terribly long!!! She feels someone tapping on her shoulder. She whirls around and sees a man in a bright red cape! It's Superman! He points to her and points to the top of the tower. Suddenly, Valerie feels herself flying through the cool air. She lands on top of the tower! She looks down and sees the lights of Paris glittering below her. Valerie is very, very happy.

What's going on with these "sense-sational" stories? They're just the usual in a foreign language classroom that employs all the senses, engages the mind, activates humor, and involves students physically and emotionally as they learn vocabulary and grammar structures in an exciting context. This new approach to foreign language acquisition draws on many of the habits of mind, and it is nothing like the traditional way many of us studied foreign languages when we were in high school.

THE GRAMMATICAL APPROACH

Many of us remember when foreign languages were taught using a purely grammatical approach. Students received vocabulary lists to memorize, and sometimes they were reinforced with pictures or examples of the words. Grammar structures and verb tenses were taught by presentations, explanations, note taking, worksheets, and drill. All of these benefited few, and only a small percentage of students mastered them.

None of these methods involved the whole student. The language didn't come alive, and students didn't engage their senses, emotions, or bodies. Yet foreign language teachers continued to teach this way. They reasoned that they had learned successfully in this manner, and their students should succeed, too. Over the years, the number of students who continued with language classes decreased, until only a tiny fraction remained in the higher levels. Schools in effect limited their foreign language programs to students with the most well-developed study skills, and many assumed that others couldn't—and wouldn't—be successful.

A NEW APPROACH

Fortunately, using all the senses has become more common in foreign language teaching, and this approach has enabled students with a variety of abilities to succeed. Essentially, we all acquired our first language through using all our senses. Studies show that even before a child is born, the child feels and recognizes the rhythm of language. After a baby is born, the baby continues to see, hear, and feel language without, of course, being expected to produce it until the baby is ready.

When a child utters that first word, parents are ecstatic—even if the word is pronounced incorrectly! Few parents would even consider correcting a baby saying "dada" instead of "daddy." Yet as the child grows older, much language acquisition is through response to commands.

"Come here and give Grandma a kiss!" exclaims Grandma as she points to her cheek. Soon the baby notices that a kiss leads to a hug and squeals of delight from Grandma.

"Don't pull the kitty's tail! Pet her nicely, like this," says Mom as she takes the baby's hand and shows the proper way to pet a cat. Soon the child learns that the soft, fluffy thing that sleeps on the couch all day is called a kitty.

"Stay away from the stove! It's hot, hot, hot!" Dad warns as he cooks spaghetti. The baby soon associates the steam coming from the pot with Dad's warning of danger and that hot can hurt.

At this stage, the child is receptive to language in all its forms: spoken and unspoken, through expressions, emotions, and body movements. The child receives "comprehensible input," which is stored for the day when the child is ready to use the language to communicate verbally (Krashen & Terrell, 1983).

AN ACTIVE, CREATIVE START

In my foreign language classroom at Dixon High School in Dixon, California, I use commands that require listening and responding with understanding. I find that they are a useful starting point in teaching vocabulary and advancing the acquisition of a second language. Beginning students are asked to respond to commands, but they are not asked to produce spoken language (Ray & Seely, 1997).

I try to make this stage as active, vivid, humorous, and creative as possible. I say much more than just "touch your nose, touch your toes, stand up, sit down, look to the left, look to the right." The commands should be as lively as the teacher can make them (Ray & Seely, 1997):

- "Put your belly button on the ceiling and wave at it!"
- "Point to the teacher and laugh."
- "Go to McDonalds and buy a hamburger. Smell the hamburger, and take a big bite. Yum!"
- "Kiss the floor."
- "Throw the ball at the door."
- "Put the teacher in the trash can."

Students receive comprehensible input, react to the commands, and store vocabulary in their long-term memory because they are reacting to it physically. They're having a great time in class, too. At this point, no written production is expected, a point you may have to explain to parents.

Eventually, students need and are ready to hear, see, and acquire vocabulary in a specific context. Now they are ready to work with short stories, like the ones at the beginning of this chapter. These stories make the second language come alive (Ray & Seely, 1997), and they are designed to engage the senses. For example, the story of the hot salsa engages the sense of taste. Katerina's snoring story engages listening. Valerie's Paris adventure engages visual, tactile, and kinesthetic senses.

Before asking students to create such a story, the teacher presents main words or phrases to be included. Each of these "language chunks" is assigned a physical motion that, after repeated practice, the student will associate with the new vocabulary (Ray & Seely, 1997). A hand up to the ear can indicate hearing, fingers pinching the nose can symbolize stinking, and an arm thrust forward can mean throwing. Students also benefit when you give them something in their first language to connect with the new word. For example, if you're teaching the Spanish word for "to think," *pensar*, children can draw forth past knowledge to relate it to "pensive" or "penny for your thoughts." After students practice the movements, the teacher presents the story, and students act it out, using the physical motions (Ray & Seely, 1997).

In the story about Juan and the mislabeled salsa, the students empathize with Juan. They intentionally use the motions and the new vocabulary to buy, open, smell, taste, react in horror to, and be rescued from the extra hot salsa that Juan brings from the store. Naturally there is no salsa, but the students pretend to hold the salsa in their hands as they visualize and "taste" it. They also internalize the new vocabulary associated with the salsa in the story.

When acting out the situation about Katerina and the snorer, the class snores loudly and rudely with great delight. Students use the sense of hearing, and they are annoyed by the excessive snoring. The police tear into the classroom and yank the snorer away. Katerina finally gets some sleep, and all the while the students employ reflexive verbs without even realizing it.

In the third story, students playing the lucky Valerie finally fly through the air feeling the cool Paris air on their faces. They see the glittering lights in the world's most romantic city. The next step is for students to tell the story to each other in pairs, using the main words and phrases as a guide (Ray & Seely, 1997). It's a lot of fun watching students try to draw forth a word or expression using motion to aid their memory.

Several other steps are designed to motivate students' thinking in the target language and to improve their spoken proficiency. One of these involves questioning techniques designed to elicit the students' use of the vocabulary and to check their comprehension of the facts presented in the story. Students call out answers to questions. The questions can be in true/false form, such as, "The salsa is blue, right?" to which they will say, "No! It's red!" Or, the students may be challenged to choose among several possibilities: "Is the salsa blue, white, or red?" Of course, they will shout, "Red!" Finally, the questions may be designed to have the students produce facts. For example, I simply may ask, "The color of the salsa is. . . ?" Once again, the answer is, "Red!" (Ray & Seely, 1997).

The language in the stories can be serious or ludicrous, as long as it provides students with usable vocabulary. At this point, the whole world, figuratively speaking, can be brought into the classroom. Students will best remember and enjoy any words or phrases that engage the senses:

• A cuddly kitten biting your finger with its teeny, tiny teeth.
• The acrid smell of cigarettes on a crowded European train.
• The mouthwatering aroma of barbecuing steaks coming from the house next door.
• An air conditioner that breaks when the temperature is 100 degrees.
• The Spanish teacher listening to the Beatles when the students prefer the Spice Girls.

Absolutely any vocabulary can be acquired in the foreign language classroom through visualizing, imagining, using appropriate props, and using a physical action to effect long-term retention. The best part, of course, is students' enthusiasm and their realization that they really are learning. They are excited and proud when they can draw from their memory a word or expression several months after a lesson, with the help of the motions.

All teachers, regardless of subject area, can enhance their students' learning by using this habit of mind: gathering data through all senses. It is my hope that through the sensory processes of role playing, moving, touching, smelling, tasting, and envisioning, students can enhance their self-knowledge, become aware of how they learn best, and apply that knowledge in their continuous, lifelong learning.

REFERENCES

Krashen, S. D., & Terrell, T. D. (1983). *The natural approach: Language acquisition in the classroom.* Hayward, CA: Alemany Press.

Ray, B., & Seely, C. (1997). *Fluency through TPR storytelling.* Berkeley, CA: The Command Performance Language Institute.

12

ENHANCING READING COMPREHENSION INSTRUCTION THROUGH HABITS OF MIND

THOMMIE DePINTO PIERCY

One day as I dropped off my eldest son at school, I turned to my 6-year-old son and said, "This is the school I went to, Ian!"

He replied, "Was that when life was black and white?"

By this time in my life, I no longer felt compelled to figure out everything for my children. So instead of immediately trying to help him understand why our old family photos were not in color, I honored Ian's question with silence. Once at home, I told him that I thought his question was very special, and he might want to save it in his journal. Later, as I made holiday cookies with brightly colored M&Ms, Ian sat at the kitchen table writing. He told me, "Mom, it's like these cookies. On the outside they're in color, but on the inside, they're still all black and white."

Ian had gotten inside his question.

We cannot give our students memorable conversations with their parents. We cannot give them a caring family that listens and cares about all their questions or a home warmed by cookies. But we can honor their questions in school. We can guide them to treasure their own thoughts, and we can help them believe that thoughts are too special to be forgotten.

In particular, when students read literature, the thoughts and questions they generate *during* reading can help them dig deeper into the meaning of the story. The habits of mind also support this comprehension. This chapter addresses the question, "What reading instruction do we provide readers when comprehension is *not* breaking down?" I focus on using the habits

137

of metacognition and questioning as powerful strategies to deepen under-standing. Imagine students having strategies to extend their understandings when comprehension is going well, just as they have "fix-it" strategies when meaning is breaking down. What would student behaviors look and sound like if children acquired and used the habits of mind *during* reading comprehension?

METACOGNITIVE ANCHORING

Metacognitive anchoring is a strategy to move comprehension instruction to a deeper level by asking questions and thinking about thinking. Developed by Frank Lyman, this strategy suggests that students explicitly ask, "How should my mind work?" while they are reading. How do you teach this kind of metacognitive anchoring to young students? It sounds like this in the model version of instruction, as students ask themselves these questions while they read:

• What does this remind me of, or how is it similar to something else I know?
• Why did this happen, or what caused this?
• What evidence supports this?
• How valid are these assumptions?
• Is this ethical or right? How should I evaluate this?
• Do I believe what is being said here? Is the writer trying to persuade me?
• What point of view is guiding these statements?

Teaching students to ask, "How should my mind work?" also helps them to comprehend more deeply and more successfully. Students find themselves saying something like, "Oh! That means. . . ." This is an exam-ple of a translating statement, which students use to restate the passage for comprehension.

A teacher who models metacognitive anchoring encourages students to use similar kinds of questions. As a result, students comprehend text beyond the literal level and global stance, generate questions, and respond to writing prompts. For example, Megan Tracey, a 3rd grade teacher at Friendship Valley Elementary School in Westminster, Maryland, explains to her students as she reads that she finds herself in conversation with the author. *During* reading, she asks herself, "How should my mind work?" This question anchors her thinking inside the text *as* she is reading.

One way Tracey keeps her thinking anchored within the passage is by writing thoughts in the margin. We refer to these thoughts as margin metacognition. This type of writing slows down the processing of text, providing rich time to generate connections and new thoughts and comprehend at a deeper level. Tracey explains that writing in the margins helps to share thoughts back and forth with the author. Many times she generates questions about what is happening in the text. These questions and thoughts may be entered into her journal later as seeds for writing.

Tracey cautions students that even though she is writing in her book, she would never scribble in it. She highlights particular words because they create special images in her mind. On a portion of the text enlarged on an overhead projector, Tracey demonstrates the reflective purposes for highlighting. She highlights words that create questions she has not thought about before, power words that make strong images in her mind, and words that are humorous or remind her of herself.

MODELING METACOGNITIVE ANCHORING

Students must be given a chance to try out metacognitive anchoring by writing in the margins and highlighting passages for specific purposes. With practice time in class, students are soon able to apply comprehension strategies independently. Figure 12.1 (see p. 140) shows how a student modeled metacognitive anchoring in grade 5, following the process Tracey described.

My Life in Dog Years, a series of four books by Gary Paulsen, provides developmental readers excellent, affordable literature in which they can write in the margins with the margin metacognition strategy. Then they can keep their own copies as adults do. Articles from publications such as *Time for Kids* are especially well designed for instruction on margin metacognition because they are available at all reading levels, including the Big Book format.

As the text and students' thinking connect, the student determines which comprehension strategy is needed. This transformation from text to acquired meaning is comprehension.

Students display an understanding and ownership when they use the strategy of margin metacognition, which they refer to as their "M & M's." At last, teachers can *see* their students' amazing inner dialogue in these margins. Figure 12.2 (see p. 141) shows how students use the metacognitive questioning chart to "unpack" their thinking by reflecting upon their thoughts and questions written in the margins (DePinto Piercy, 1998).

FIGURE 12.1

Student's Modeling of Metacognitive Anchoring

Text Highlighted by Student (Text from *Dirk*, by G. Pausen)	Student's Meta-cognitive Questions Asked *During* Reading	Student's Explanation of Why Question Was Asked
When Olaf reached out to pet him, Dirk actually—this was the first time I'd seen it—wagged his tail. He'd found a home.	Do you think Dirk and the guy who owned him were made for each other? Do you think they knew they were?	I asked this question because I thought it was strange the way Dirk and the farmer bonded.
As I reached the bottom and my foot hit the ground, I heard a low growl: It was a rumble, so full of menace and threat that it stopped me cold, my foot frozen in midair.	Did Dirk ever have another owner?	I asked this because of the way he acted when people came around him.

Students use the chart *during* reading and review their margin metacognition notes *after* reading. The middle column of the chart asks students to identify the type of thinking they incorporated in their question. They identify this thinking with symbols, which come from Lyman's question/response cuing strategy (Lyman & McTighe, 1991). These symbols are visual cues for seven different types of thinking used for generating questions and responding to prompts. The chart also helps students collect the fluid nature of thought on the flatlands of paper. By transferring the essence of comprehension to the metacognitive questioning chart, students reflect on their thinking, consider the questions they generated while they were reading the text, and more importantly, ponder why three specific questions were generated.

As students come to understand that comprehension includes asking questions *during* reading a text, they learn to respond to the questions being asked *after* reading the same text. When these students are required to respond to writing prompts on performance assessments for reading comprehension, they are able to use their metacognitive anchoring *during* reading. This *during*-reading strategy also supports students' thinking when they write responses to questions *after* reading. The following writing

FIGURE 12.2

Metacognitive Questioning Chart

My Questions *During* Reading	Type of Thinking I Used	Why I Asked This Question
When Jason walks into Mr. Henry's house, he sees a picture of a man in an Army uniform. Who do you think this man could be? Give three justifications.		This question has been sitting on my mind all day.

Source: DePinto Piercy, 1998.

prompt (Maryland State Department of Education, 1992) demonstrates the use of the metacognitive anchoring strategy for written responses:

[Writing Prompt]

In the United States today, a large number of people are moving to communities in states such as Arizona, Nevada, and Utah, where there are large areas of desert. List two things that could happen to the desert environment as more people move there.

[Student's Use of Metacognitive Anchoring]

I think what the prompt is asking me (or . . . it means that . . .) is, People moving to the desert could cause what two effects on the desert environment? I think this because the phrase "could happen to" is cause-effect thinking, so the prompt is actually asking me for two effects!

This response shows how students can take the time to translate the actual question asked. If students understand the question asked, they are better prepared to respond.

This strategy has more than short-term value for increasing assessment scores. Throughout their lives, students will need to understand and work with a variety of texts and questions. If students know how to read a text and use translating phrases to grasp the meaning, they possess strategies to comprehend anything they read.

How can you provide comprehension instruction for using metacognitive anchoring? Begin modeling it yourself. For example, tell students, "I am going to ask some questions. After each question, I will rephrase it (say it differently) to make sure it is clear." Then ask several questions:

• "How would you summarize Chapter 3 of *The Trumpet of the Swan?* *I mean by that,* what are examples of the important details?"

• "What are the comparisons between *The Trumpet of the Swan* and *Charlotte's Web? I mean by that,* how would you describe the differences between the characters and the setting in each E. B. White book?"

As reading and writing strategies settle into the homes of students' minds, children begin to understand that comprehension strategies belong to them. Students begin to use these strategies all the time because they know that thinking is important in all subjects, even when they are not in directed reading groups. At the same time, students develop habits of mind that are essential to finding deeper meaning in any text: applying past knowledge to new situations, persisting, questioning and posing problems, using metacognition, and thinking flexibly. There are a rich variety of before and after reading strategies. Readers, however, cannot be left alone *during* reading to travel through the heavy traffic of richly written literature. The habits of mind guide them in their journey. Providing comprehension instruction *during* reading cannot be overlooked. We simply need to get into the habit of doing it!

REFERENCES

DePinto Piercy, T. (1998). *The effects of multistrategy instruction upon reading comprehension.* Unpublished doctoral dissertation, University of Maryland, College Park.

Lyman, F. Jr., & McTighe, J. (1991). Cueing thinking in the classroom: The promise of theory-embedded tools. In A. Costa (Ed.), *Developing minds: A resource book for teaching thinking* (Rev. ed., Vol. 1, pp. 243–250). Alexandria, VA: Association for Supervision and Curriculum Development.

Maryland State Department of Education. (1992). The Maryland school performance assessment program criterion-referenced tests. Baltimore, MD: Author.

13

HABITS OF MIND AS CHARACTER EDUCATION

CURTIS SCHNORR

In recent years, schools have been challenged to teach character education, which encompasses moral values and good citizenship. This charge sent many districts searching for programs to implement their state and local mandates. Though they found a variety of options to meet their needs, I believe their search should have started—and ended—with the habits of mind.

Why should thinking be the foundation for a character education program? I have a better question: Why *shouldn't* thinking be the foundation? Successful character education is grounded in thoughtful processes. Schools need to develop climates that support and foster these thinking processes, just as they support development of students who are productive citizens with strong character. The habits of mind can help achieve all these goals.

THE NEED FOR CHARACTER DEVELOPMENT

In *Educating for Character*, Thomas Likona (1991) observes, "Until recently, calls for school reform have focused on academic achievement. Now we know that character development is needed as well" (p. 22). Likona bases his arguments on troubling trends among youth. He also bases his arguments on the belief that if schools want to do one thing to improve teachers' lives, they will make moral education—including the creation of a civil, humane school community—the center of school life.

A recent brochure from the Maryland State Department of Education (1998) supports this idea: "Character education is not a program—it's a way of life. Character education will come in a variety of forms. The ideal approach should be to infuse character education into the daily operation of the school" (p. 1). Elias and colleagues (1997) concur with this idea: "Social and emotional competence is the ability to understand, manage, and express the social/emotional aspects of one's life in ways that enable the successful management of life tasks such as learning, forming relationships, solving everyday problems, and adapting to complex demands of growth and development" (p. 2).

Let there be no confusion: Development of a classroom and school environment that is safe and orderly for both students and teachers is at the root of character education. As Alfie Kohn (1996) observes, "How students act in class is so intertwined with curricular content that it may be a folly even to talk about classroom management or discipline as a field unto itself" (p. 21). Kohn further asks, "How can we deny that the way children act in a classroom is significantly related to their interest in what they've been given to do? Tapping and extending that interest takes time and talent, patience and skill and even courage" (p. 21). Curwin and Mendler (1988) summarize this concept well: "Every decision affecting behavior management also affects instruction" (p. 20).

We want students to use what they learn to solve all kinds of problems: new *and* old. Many school administrators agree that the majority of office visits occurs because students fail to solve problems in a thoughtful manner. This concern leads to another important question: How do human beings "behave intelligently," and how does this affect character education and behavior management? I believe our work at Friendship Valley Elementary School in Westminster, Maryland, answers both these questions.

CHARACTER EDUCATION AT FRIENDSHIP VALLEY

Over the past six years, Friendship Valley's enrollment increased almost 30 percent, yet office referrals for discipline did not rise proportionally. In fact, behavior referrals still declined when student enrollment went to a school high of more than 750 students. We believe the most important factor contributing to this decline was development of a thoughtful student body that (1) used intelligent behaviors and (2) took time to think before taking action.

Students have learned to stop and think before they act because teachers and administrators at Friendship Valley constantly ask these questions:

• What intelligent behavior did you *not* use that resulted in a classroom or school problem?

• What intelligent behavior could you use to prevent future incidents?

Students with office referrals are asked to complete a problem-solving sheet that includes those same two questions. Depending on their grade level, students have to respond either in writing or orally to a school administrator concerning their use (or lack of use) of the habits of mind. Following are some of our reflections on the habits of mind gained through these interactions with students.

Persisting. (Stick to it) Students who are persistent do not give up easily. They stick to an activity until the end. Students exhibiting persistence are less likely to stray off task, and they are less likely to interrupt the learning environment for others. As students increase their persistence, they focus more on thinking, and they are less likely to cause classroom and school disruptions.

Managing impulsivity. (Take your time) Teachers encourage students to use "think time" before offering an answer. Students need to practice using think time to decrease their impulsivity in everything they do. Consider how many times impulsive students interrupt the learning environment. How many office referrals are the result of students' impulsivity? As students reduce their impulsivity, they are less likely to enter into arguments with others, and they are more likely to focus on the task at hand.

Listening with understanding and empathy. (Understand others) When we take time to listen to others, we take time to understand them. When we understand others, we are less likely to get into disagreements. We need to teach students how to listen to others. Listening provides the opportunity to empathize with others and to understand their point of view.

Thinking flexibly. (Look at it another way) Students often have difficulty envisioning alternatives. Without alternative points of view, they become rigid in their thinking. Rigid thinking prevents students from generating open-minded responses to various social situations. Teachers and administrators need to provide students opportunities for practicing and demonstrating flexible thinking, which fosters a tolerance of others.

Thinking about thinking (metacognition). (Know your knowing) When students become aware of their own thinking, they begin to understand that their way may not always be the best or only way. Students who take time to understand their own thinking develop an appreciation for and understanding of the thinking and actions of others.

Striving for accuracy. (Look over your work) Students who take the time to check for accuracy are less likely to act impulsively. They check their facts

145

and the sources of information before taking action. Checking for accuracy deters students from responding to rumors and false accusations. Checking for accuracy also provides students necessary think time.

Questioning and posing problems. (Work it out) Taking the time to question and problem solve prevents student disputes and disagreements. Students who problem solve become more thoughtful, respectful citizens. Problem solvers are less impulsive in their actions and responses to others.

Applying past knowledge to new situations. (Use what you learn) By using prior knowledge, students are less prone to repeat poor choices or mistakes. Students using prior knowledge learn from their past experiences. They exhibit a greater sense of thoughtfulness as they encounter problems and difficulties with others.

Thinking and communicating with clarity and precision. (Be clear) Students who develop a precision of language and thought clearly communicate their ideas, intentions, and actions to others. Clear communication eliminates many misunderstandings. Precision of language also can prevent many disputes that occur in the classroom, on the playground, and in the cafeteria.

Gathering data through all senses. (Use natural pathways) Students who use all their senses take the time to examine issues from all viewpoints. They listen to problems, but they also seek out confirming information visually before taking positive action.

Creating, imagining, innovating. (See things differently) Creative students solve differences in a more thoughtful manner. They seek alternate solutions to classroom and school issues. Creative problem solvers seek alternate solutions to problems they encounter during the school day. They resort less to classroom and playground disruptions.

Responding with wonderment and awe. (Have fun working it out) By enjoying problem solving, students do not let themselves get burdened by life's little problems. They see problems as opportunities to enhance their thinking skills.

Taking responsible risks. (Seek adventure with responsibility) Students often take irresponsible risks on the playground and in the classroom. This endangers the safety, well-being, and personal space of others around them. Responsible risk takers plan and think carefully before taking risks in any situation.

Finding humor. (Pursue joy and laughter) Students who know the value of humor do not let themselves get overburdened with life's little problems. Instead, they seek pleasure in the world around them. They learn to use humor intelligently to diffuse classroom and playground problems.

Thinking interdependently. (Work together) When students work, plan, and think together, they not only expand their thinking, but they also help to develop a strong learning environment. By working together, students develop an appreciation for the talents and skills of those around them. They begin to value their classmates' contributions.

Remaining open to continuous learning. (Keep your mind growing) Teachers need to model the importance of lifelong learning. Students need to see teachers fascinated by the joy and wonderment of new learning. As they develop this habit, students will remain open to the contributions, thoughts, and teaching from those around them.

Costa (1991) observes that the search for intelligent life will lead to students who "display cognizant and compassionate behavior toward other life forms as they are able to understand the need for protecting their environment, respecting the roles and values of other human beings and perceiving the delicate worth, uniqueness, and relationships of everything and everyone they encounter" (p. 30). The goal of any character education should be the creation of compassionate, thoughtful, humane students. Above all, thoughtful students are the key to fostering learning environments that place a premium on thinking, which results in intelligent student behavior.

REFERENCES

Costa, A. (1991). *The school as a home for the mind.* Palatine, IL: Skylight Publishing.

Curwin, R., & Mendler, A. (1988). *Discipline with dignity.* Alexandria, VA: Association for Supervision and Curriculum Development.

Elias, M., Zins, J., Weissberg, R., Frey, K., Greenberg, M., Haynes, N., Kessler, R., Schwab-Stone, M., & Shriver, T. (1997). *Promoting social and emotional learning: Guidelines for educators.* Alexandria, VA: Association for Supervision and Curriculum Development.

Kohn, A. (1996). *Beyond discipline: From compliance to community.* Alexandria, VA: Association for Supervision and Curriculum Development.

Likona, T. (1991). *Educating for character.* New York: Bantam Books.

Maryland State Department of Education. (1998). *Character education* [brochure]. Baltimore, MD: Author.

14

GETTING STARTED

ARTHUR L. COSTA, BENA KALLICK, AND LISA DAVIS

Awareness is the first step toward owning the habits of mind. Both students and adults have to engage with the habits before they can use them. They must be able to state them in their own words, recognize where they have seen the behaviors in their own experiences, and imagine where and how they might use the behaviors in their own lives. Many teachers have started to build awareness of the habits of mind using the activities in this chapter. This chapter offers a compilation of many ideas collected from around the world, with particular recognition of the work of Lisa Davis, a teacher at West Orchard School in Chappaqua, New York.

IN THEIR OWN TERMS

Some teachers start work with the habits of mind by letting students define the habits in their own terms. Group students in pairs or threes to complete this activity.

First, ask each group to work on one or two habits. They should respond to the following statements on large sheets of paper with magic markers or crayons:

- Write the name of the habit you are defining on the top of the paper.
- Say the meaning of the habit in your own words.
- Give examples of what the habit looks like and sounds like in action.
- Create a slogan for the habit.
- Create a logo for the habit.

After students have responded, they can hang their charts on the wall to create a gallery of the habits of mind. As students share their work with one another, they gain more insights into the concepts behind them. Students also gain insights by reading descriptions of the habits of mind (for example, see Chapter 2 and the word splash activity).

Other teachers have helped students understand the habits of mind through a jigsaw activity. Count off so students are grouped in threes. Each group then reads about two habits in this "home" group. Next, have students regroup into "expert" groups. Here they will become authorities on the meaning of two habits. The expert group must find a way to teach the habits to the home group. Then they return to the home group and teach the habits they have learned. Continue this rotation for several days until all the habits are fully explored. In both activities, the most important aspect of the exercise is how students (and perhaps adults) restate, define, and operationalize the habits.

INTRODUCING THE HABITS

In one middle school we've visited, a team of 8th grade teachers divided the habits so that each teacher covered four of them. During the first week of school, each teacher introduced four habits. Students were asked to give each habit its own definition and to create logos for it. These logos were cut out and formed into mobiles that hung in their common hallway.

In a high school we've visited, the entire 9th grade agreed to focus on one habit a week for the first two months of school. They believed that as they entered high school, they needed to be more aware of the habits necessary for successful learning. As the students built their definitions, they placed them in a notebook. They gradually familiarized themselves with the habits of mind, and soon they could describe where the habits were evident in their performance.

In a 4th grade classroom we've visited, the teacher first introduced her students to the concept of thinking and then gradually built to the habits of mind. She and her colleagues defined the teacher as someone who coaches and consults with students rather than someone who lectures from the front of the room. Teaching in a facilitator's role results in a room filled with visual evidence of students' thinking and shared decision making.

Consider this example from Lisa Davis's classroom. In the beginning of the school year, Davis asks her students, "Can you sit exactly like Auguste Rodin's 'The Thinker'? What do you think he is thinking about?" The discussion that follows quickly evolves to the question, "What is thought?" After gazing at a large print of Rodin's sculpture on the easel, students scatter around the room in an effort to show their thinking poses.

At the end of their active discussion, Davis challenges students to write their ideas on "What is thinking and what does it look like?" At another time, to engage metaphorical thinking, she asks, "How is thinking like a river?" Finally, she culminates these opening activities with a thinking gallery. Each student receives a block of clay to sculpt into a representation of the idea of thinking. After the pieces are baked, the permanent sculptures are placed in the thinking gallery, celebrated, and discussed. A year in the thoughtful classroom has begun.

CREATING SIGNIFICANT CONTEXT

The habits of mind need a significant context. Once students understand that they are to create and be responsible for their community of learning, they must also learn the habits of mind necessary to ensure that the community operates in an open, fair, democratic way. Lisa Davis begins this process with a question: "What does an effective learner do?" This query sets students off on an adventure that results in development of a classroom mission statement.

First, Davis brainstorms the question with students, discussing their vision for success as a community of learners. Together they examine what it means to be interdependent. They analyze mission statements collected from parents' workplaces, and they talk about and record their ideas about possible classroom mission statements.

Next, students craft their ideas into a final student mission statement. One mission statement looked like this: "It is the mission of the Community of Learners, a multi-age team, to come to school open and eager to learn by having a positive attitude, being respectful, listening, cooperating, keeping an open mind, being persistent, thinking critically, helping each other, trying hard every day, and being a leader when called upon."

With a sense of pride and accomplishment, students hang their mission statement in a prominent place in the classroom. They use the statement as a reference point throughout the year, and all students feel a sense of ownership.

A COMMON LANGUAGE

One day in late fall, Tommy came in from recess, face red, hair disheveled, and backpack dragging. "Boy, that Ryan!" he said, glaring at a fellow student known for his temper. "He sure doesn't manage his impulsivity!"

150

One of Davis's main resources for developing a common language of the habits of mind is the way she introduces them. When first introducing the habits to students, Davis gives each child a cardboard stand with a habits-of-mind bookmark. Students can then look at the habits of mind throughout the day. Having the habits of mind in full view also helps her weave them into a variety of subjects and activities. Within a short time, students use the language of thinking with ease and understanding.

"Boys and girls," she asks, "what habits of mind do you think Billy is using in this chapter of *Where the Red Fern Grows?*"

Or, she may probe for metacognition: "Denise, can you tell us about your thinking process as you figured out that math problem?"

DEVELOPING A T-CHART

Before starting group work, discuss with students the idea that part of the reason for working together is to produce better-informed, more refined, and more creative work. The expectation is that it will be "mind" work, and students must therefore have a set of "mindful" ways of working.

Introduce one or two habits that best fit the nature of the work to be done. One strategy teachers use is a T-chart in which students see how it would look and sound if they used the habits. Figure 14.1 (see p. 152) shows such a chart.

This list is generated and used during the group process for self-monitoring and group monitoring. At the end of the process, be certain to debrief students on the use of the habits as well as the quality of the work that was accomplished.

USING THE HABITS FOR GOAL SETTING

Many teachers have found it beneficial to have students write and assess their learning goals using the habits of mind as a springboard for goal setting. To guide students through the process of goal setting, Lisa Davis asks students to

- Write a specific goal.
- Predict the outcome of the goal.
- List three ways to achieve the goal.
- Seek parental approval of the goal.

FIGURE 14.1

Listening with Understanding and Empathy

Looks Like	Sounds Like
Leans forward to speaker.	Paraphrases: "So what you are saying is . . . ."
Nods head.	Asks clarifying questions: "I want to understand what you meant by . . . ."
Makes eye contact.	Silent when speaker is presenting material.

One of Davis's students wrote the following goal: "I will check for accuracy and precision when doing written work. The outcome of my goal is that the quality of my written work will improve. Three ways to achieve this goal are (1) I will use class time wisely so I can spend more time on my assignment; (2) I will read over and edit my work; (3) I will have one other person read my work and have that person make editing suggestions."

STUDENT SELF-ASSESSMENT

Have students generate a list of descriptors for the habits of mind at the beginning of the school year, soon after they have defined and described them. This list helps them hold the habits in their minds, apply them to their work, and assess their performance throughout the year or semester. Figure 14.2 shows a checklist developed by the students in Lisa Davis's classroom.

Introducing the habits of mind in a classroom often means changing the way the classroom functions. Introducing the habits may also imply that students take a larger share of the responsibility for setting up the learning environment. Students can practice the habits of mind as they

• Define the purpose of their classroom through a mission statement.
• Describe how they intend to operate within that classroom individually and as a group.
• Define how they will conduct themselves as thoughtful learners.

FIGURE 14.2
Student Self-Assessment Checklist of Critical Thinking

Name: _____   Date: _____

What Does a Critical Thinker Look Like?	Most of the Time	Sometimes	Not Yet
1. Is persistent and persevering. I stay on task. I use a variety of strategies to solve problems. I might say, "Don't show me. Let me figure it out." I complete my tasks or projects.			
2. Has decreased impulsivity. I listen to instructions before I begin. I ask questions if I don't understand. I think before I act. I develop a plan before I start work. I accept suggestions to improve my work. I listen to other points of view.			
3. Works accurately and precisely. I take time to be precise. I check that my information is accurate. I review the requirements on assignments. I edit and revise to make my writing clear. I check that my work matches the criteria.			
4. Listens with understanding. I listen carefully to others and value their ideas. I respond appropriately. I build on others' ideas.			
5. Is flexible in thinking. I try to understand both sides of an issue. I consider all viewpoints in solving a problem.			
6. Has awareness of own thinking. I am able to list the steps in my plan of action. I can describe what I know and what I need to know. I can evaluate my plan. I can explain the steps in my thinking. I can tell how thinking about thinking helps me.			

FIGURE 14.2—*continued*
Student Self-Assessment Checklist of Critical Thinking

Name: _____   Date: _____

What Does a Critical Thinker Look Like?	Most of the Time	Sometimes	Not Yet
7. Asks questions and solves problems. I ask questions and am curious. I think of a lot of ways to do things. I gather information and figure out what it means. I can think of more than one solution to a problem. I can explain why my thinking makes good sense.			
8. Uses past knowledge in new situations. I use my past learning in new situations. I can see how two different ideas are connected.			
9. Thinks creatively. I am willing to try new approaches. I like to think about things and wonder about them. I can think of ideas that are really unusual. I add a lot to my ideas and to others' ideas. I stick to my task and finish the job.			

Source: Students in Lisa Davis's class, West Orchard Elementary School, Chappaqua, New York.

We can change schools one teacher at a time; we can change schools one classroom at a time; we can change schools one building at a time. But change we must if we are to move successfully through an age that requires critical and creative thinking as never before. As Edward de Bono has observed, "If you never change your mind, why have one?"

ACKNOWLEDGMENTS

W̲e wish to express our appreciation to the many contributors to this series of books. The descriptions of their experiences, lessons, implementation strategies, vignettes, and artwork are what give meaning, expression, and practicality to the habits of mind. To them we are eternally grateful.

We wish to thank John O'Neil, Nancy Modrak, Julie Houtz, Margaret Oosterman, and other members of the ASCD editorial staff who encouraged and guided us throughout this project. Our gratitude is expressed to our editor, René Bahrenfuss, for her flexibility, her striving for accuracy, and her persistence. We are appreciative of the artistic talents of Georgia McDonald and other ASCD design staff for the habits of mind icons. Without their attention to detail, striving for perfection, and creative imagination, this series could not have come to fruition.

We also wish to thank our assistants, Kim Welborn and Carol Hunsicker, whose secretarial skills and computer wizardry behind the scenes kept us organized and in communication with each other and with all the authors.

We pay particular tribute to Bena's husband, Charles, and Art's wife, Nancy, who tolerated our time away from them. Their love, encouragement, and understanding provided the support base for our success.

Finally, we wish to acknowledge the many teachers, administrators, and parents in the numerous schools and communities throughout the United States and abroad who have adopted and implemented the habits of mind and have found them a meaningful way to organize learning. The future world will be a more thoughtful, compassionate, and cooperative place because of their dedication to cultivating the habits of mind in students and modeling them in their own behavior.

TEACHER, SCHOOL, AND DISTRICT ACKNOWLEDGMENTS

We would like to thank the many teachers, schools, and districts throughout the United States who contributed to the writing of this book. Their combined efforts helped us develop a comprehensive presentation of the 16 habits of mind.

California
Foreign Language Department
Dixon High School
Dixon Unified School District
Dixon, California

Marilyn Tabor
Irvine Unified School District
Irvine, California

Maryland
Megan Tracey
Friendship Valley Elementary
 School
Carroll County School District
Westminster, Maryland

Minnesota
Marcy Open School
Minneapolis, Minnesota

Hidden Valley Elementary School
Burnsville, Minnesota

New York
Lisa Davis
West Orchard Elementary School
Chappaqua, New York

Team of 6th Grade Social Studies
 Teachers (Nancy Patton,
 Susan Pereira, Susan Sage,
 Sam Slotnick)
New Paltz Middle School
New Paltz, New York

Bronxville School
Bronxville, New York

Texas
Cathy Earl
Danbury High School
Danbury, Texas

Washington
Tahoma School District
Maple Valley, Washington

First Grade Team
Lake Wilderness Elementary
   School
Tahoma School District
Maple Valley, Washington

Wisconsin
Critical Thinking Leadership Team
   (Karen Hirsch, Pat Neudecker,
   Sue Savolainen, Jackie Belka,
   Pat Popple, Jim Erdman,
   Laurie Hittman, Sharon Giles,
   Ilene Doty, Lynn McNish,
   Don Johnson, Deb Hansen,
   Gerry Holt, Stephanie Rowe)
Eau Claire Area School District
Eau Claire, Wisconsin

INDEX

ABOUT THE AUTHORS

Arthur L. Costa is an emeritus professor of education at California State University, Sacramento, and codirector of the Institute for Intelligent Behavior in Cameron Park, California. He has been a classroom teacher, a curriculum consultant, and an assistant superintendent for instruction, as well as the director of educational programs for the National Aeronautics and Space Administration. He has made presentations and conducted workshops in all 50 states, as well as in Mexico, Central and South America, Canada, Australia, New Zealand, Africa, Europe, Asia, and the Islands of the South Pacific.

Costa has written numerous articles and books, including *Techniques for Teaching Thinking* (with Larry Lowery), *The School as a Home for the Mind*, and *Cognitive Coaching: A Foundation for Renaissance Schools* (with Robert Garmston). He is editor of *Developing Minds: A Resource Book for Teaching Thinking* and coeditor (with Rosemarie Liebmann) of the Process as Content Trilogy: *Envisioning Process as Content, Supporting the Spirit of Learning*, and *The Process-Centered School*.

Active in many professional organizations, Costa served as president of the California Association for Supervision and Curriculum Development and as national president of the Association for Supervision and Curriculum Development, 1988–89. Costa can be reached at Search Models Unlimited, P.O. Box 362, Davis, CA 95617-0362; phone/fax: 530-756-7872; e-mail: artcosta@aol.com.

Bena Kallick is a private consultant providing services to school districts, state departments of education, professional organizations, and public agencies throughout the United States and internationally. Kallick received her doctorate in educational evaluation at Union Graduate School. Her areas of focus include group dynamics, creative and critical thinking, and alternative assessment strategies in the classroom. Her written work includes *Literature to Think About* (a whole language curriculum published with Weston Woods Studios), *Changing Schools into Communities for Thinking,* and *Assessment in the Learning Organization* (coauthored with Arthur Costa).

Formerly a teachers' center director, Kallick also created a children's museum based on problem solving and invention. She was the coordinator of a high school alternative designed for at-risk students. She is cofounder of Technology Pathways, a company dedicated to providing easy-to-use software that helps integrate and make sense of data from curriculum, instruction, and assessment. Kallick's teaching appointments have included Yale University School of Organization and Management, University of Massachusetts Center for Creative and Critical Thinking, and Union Graduate School. She is on the board of Jobs for the Future. Kallick can be reached at 12 Crooked Mile Rd., Westport, CT 06880; phone/fax: 203-227-7261; e-mail: bkallick@aol.com.

Gina Celeste Costa has been a Spanish teacher and counselor at Dixon High School in Dixon, California, since 1983. She was a mentor teacher in 1991. With her department, Costa is currently working on developing a curriculum for her beginning and midlevel courses based on Total Physical Response Storytelling. She also teaches adult education Spanish classes in Woodland, California. Costa can be reached at gcostajones@dixonusd.org.

Lisa Davis is a professional developer in the Chappaqua Central School District. She is certified by the National Board for Professional Teaching Standards and is a graduate of Bank Street College of Education. Davis is currently a doctoral student in the Curriculum and Teaching Program at Teachers College, Columbia University. Davis's role as a professional developer includes working with and supporting teachers in building their repertoire of teaching techniques, experimenting with a variety of frameworks for learning, and demonstrating how to put theory into practice. In her most recent work of exploring the potential of technology and the impact it will have on teaching and learning, she helps teachers "revision" their classrooms for the future. Davis can be reached at the Chappaqua Central School District, 70 Roaring Brook Rd., Chappaqua, New York 10514; phone: 914-238-6226; e-mail: lidavis@chappaqua.k12.ny.us.

Thommie DePinto Piercy was a public school teacher in grades K–5 for 18 years. She currently teaches graduate courses in reading and writing, and she is principal of Mt. Airy Elementary School in Carroll County,

Maryland. She has published articles about integrating reading comprehension with two of the habits of mind: (1) questioning and posing problems and (2) thinking about thinking (metacognition). She based her research on this topic at the University of Maryland and was honored with the International Reading Association's (IRA) Research Award. In 1999, she chaired and presented at the IRA Convention in San Diego with Regie Routman. She has received the Bailor Award in recognition of her distinguished educational career. DePinto Piercy can be reached at P.O. Box 1228, Harpers Ferry, WV 25425; phone: 304-725-3128; e-mail: tpiercy@ccpl.carr.org.

Emilie Hard is an elementary school principal in the Tahoma School District in Maple Valley, Washington. She coauthored an integrated curriculum for the district with thinking skills and thinking habits at the core. She supports this curriculum by providing demonstration lessons, teacher inservice training, and instructional coaching in her role as principal. Hard has more than 20 years of elementary teaching experience in Oregon, Washington, and Alaska. She has also served on the Washington State Math Advisory Committee and was a member of the state's Classroom-Based Assessment Committee. Hard can be reached at the Tahoma School District Office, 25720 Maple Valley/Black Diamond Rd. SE, Maple Valley, WA 98038; phone: 425-432-4481; fax: 425-432-5792; e-mail: ehard@tahoma.wednet.edu.

David Hyerle is an author, consultant, and researcher whose work focuses on integrating content learning, thinking process instruction, and assessment. In his doctoral work at U.C. Berkeley and Harvard Graduate Schools of Education, Hyerle refined a practical language of visual tools he created called Thinking Maps®. He has written and produced professional development resource guides, videos, and software packages based on Thinking Maps as tools for student-centered learning and whole-school change. He has also published articles and the ASCD book *Visual Tools for Constructing Knowledge* (1996). His second book, *A Field Guide to Using Visual Tools*, will be published by ASCD in 2000. Hyerle can be reached at Designs for Thinking, 144 Goose Pond Rd., Lyme, NH 03768; phone/fax: 603-795-2757; e-mail: designs.thinking@valley.net.

Carol T. Lloyd has been a secondary school mathematics teacher for 23 years. She currently teaches in the Cumberland County Schools in Fayetteville, North Carolina. She has conducted staff development in thinking skills for the school system over the last eight years. Lloyd was a member of the Strategic Planning Committee for Thinking Skills in her district and helped develop and implement a training program on thinking skills for a system of 2,500 teachers. She has also presented on mathematics for regional and state conferences. Lloyd can be reached at Massey Hill Classical High School, 1062 Southern Ave., Fayetteville, NC 28306; phone: 910-485-8761; e-mail: clloyd@mhchs.ccs.k12.nc.us.

Nadine McDermott teaches vocal and general music in grades 6–12 for the Hewlett-Woodmere Public Schools in Long Island, New York. Previously, she taught grades 5–12 in the Bronxville Schools in Westchester County, New York, where she first integrated the habits of mind into her chorus rehearsals and general music classes. She has presented nationally and throughout New York State on music assessment. She currently serves on the New York State Music Association Assessment Task Force, and she is the state chairperson for Classroom Music. McDermott can be reached at 280 Mirth Dr., Valley Cottage, NY 10989; phone: 914-268-0466; e-mail: smsprin@j51.com.

David Perkins, codirector of Harvard Project Zero, is a senior research associate at the Harvard Graduate School of Education. He is the author of several books, including *Smart Schools: From Training Memories to Educating Minds* and *Outsmarting IQ: The Emerging Science of Learnable Intelligence,* and many articles. He has helped to develop instructional programs and approaches for teaching understanding and thinking, including initiatives in South Africa, Israel, and Latin America. He is a former Guggenheim Fellow. Perkins can be reached at Project Zero, Harvard Graduate School of Education, 323 Longfellow Hall, 13 Appian Way, Cambridge, MA 02138; phone: 617-495-4342; fax: 617-496-4288; e-mail: David_Perkins@pz.harvard.edu.

Kathleen C. Reilly has been teaching 10th and 12th grade English at Edgemont High School in Scarsdale, New York, for 22 years. She is a teacher-researcher, and she has adapted the habits of mind as a frame for the cumulative writing portfolios of her 10th grade students. Her research into the habits of mind and their application in her classroom was funded by grants from the Edgemont School Foundation entitled: "Metaphor, Cognition, and Critical Thinking" and "Developing Minds: Strategies to Teach for Thinking." She is a team leader with the Tri-State Standards Consortium and a staff developer with the Scarsdale Teachers Institute. Reilly can be reached at 211 Newtown Turnpike, Wilton, CT 06897; phone: 203-834-0067; fax: 203-761-9124; e-mail: KReillyCT@aol.com.

Curtis Schnorr is supervisor of elementary education and the extended enrichment program for Carroll County Public Schools in Westminster, Maryland. Previously, he was a school principal for 22 years. He spent seven years as principal at Friendship Valley Elementary School helping to create a "home for the mind." He has been a presenter at state and national conferences on incorporating the habits of mind into a school culture. Schnorr can be reached at 517 Washington Rd., Westminster, MD 21157; phone: 410-876-1807; e-mail: ctschno@k12.carr.org.

Nancy Skerritt is the assistant superintendent for teaching and learning in the Tahoma School District in Maple Valley, Washington. She has designed and published a training model for writing integrated curriculum with thinking skills and habits of mind as the core. Skerritt has conducted workshops in curriculum integration and thinking skills instruction. She is a member of the Washington State Assessment Advisory Committee, which is implementing a statewide performance-based assessment system. Before her work in curriculum development, Skerritt was a secondary language arts teacher and a counselor. Skerritt can be reached at the Tahoma School District Office, 25720 Maple Valley/Black Diamond Rd. SE, Maple Valley, WA 98038; phone: 425-432-4481; fax: 425-432-5792; e-mail: nskerrit@tahoma.wednet.edu.

RELATED ASCD RESOURCES: THINKING SKILLS

ASCD stock numbers are in parentheses.

Audiotapes

Connecting the Curriculum: Using an Integrated Interdisciplinary, Thematic Approach by T. Roger Taylor (#297093)

Dimensions of Learning by Robert J. Marzano and Debra Pickering (#295195)

Leading for Learning in the Digital Age (#200185)

Taking the Ho Hum out of Teaching: Strategies for Embedding Thinking Skills in the Curriculum by Robert Hanson and T. Robert Hanson (#200179)

Teachers as Decision Makers: Designing Integrated Curriculum (#299196)

Print Products

Design as a Catalyst for Learning by Meredith Davis, Peter Hawley, Bernard McMullan, and Gertrude Spilka (#197022)

A Different Kind of Classroom: Teaching with Dimensions of Learning by Robert J. Marzano (#61192107)

Dimensions of Learning Teacher's Manual, 2nd Edition, by Robert J. Marzano, Debra Pickering, and others (#197133)

Dimensions of Learning Trainer's Manual, 2nd Edition, by Robert J. Marzano, Debra Pickering, and others (#197134)

A New Vision for Staff Development by Dennis Sparks and Stephanie Hirsh (#197018)

Videotapes

Dimensions of Learning Videotape Package (6 tapes) (#614236)

How to Engage Students in Critical Thinking Skills ("How To" Series, Tape 8) (#400050)

For more information, visit us on the World Wide Web (http://www.ascd.org), send an e-mail message to member@ascd.org, call the ASCD Service Center (1-800-933-ASCD or 703-578-9600, then press 2), send a fax to 703-575-5400, or write to Information Services, ASCD, 1703 N. Beauregard St., Alexandria, VA 22311-1714 USA.